Steve Alisharan
BAxx 500

INSTRUCTOR'S MANUAL
S. MARK YOUNG

MANAGEMENT
ACCOUNTING

ANTHONY A. ATKINSON

University of Waterloo

RAJIV D. BANKER

University of Minnesota

ROBERT S. KAPLAN

Harvard University

S. MARK YOUNG

University of Southern California

D1406811

Prentice Hall
Englewood Cliffs, N.J. 07632

Production editor: Lynne Breitfeller
Assistant editor: Diane deCastro
Production coordinator: Ken Clinton

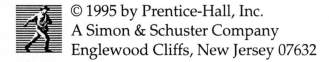 © 1995 by Prentice-Hall, Inc.
A Simon & Schuster Company
Englewood Cliffs, New Jersey 07632

All rights reserved. No part of this book may be
reproduced, in any form or by any means,
without permission in writing from the publisher.

Printed in the United States of America

10 9 8 7 6 5 4 3 2 1

ISBN 0-13-148453-2

Prentice-Hall International (UK) Limited, *London*
Prentice-Hall of Australia Pty. Limited, *Sydney*
Prentice-Hall Canada Inc., *Toronto*
Prentice-Hall Hispanoamericana, S.A., *Mexico*
Prentice-Hall of India Private Limited, *New Delhi*
Prentice-Hall of Japan, Inc., *Tokyo*
Simon & Schuster Asia Pte. Ltd., *Singapore*
Editora Prentice-Hall do Brasil, Ltda., *Rio de Janeiro*

Contents

PREFACE

Management Accounting by Atkinson, Banker, Kaplan and Young (ABKY) represents a new approach to the study of management accounting. Since the early 1980's, the field of management accounting has undergone the most significant changes over the past 40 years. The text was written to incorporate a great deal of the new knowledge that has been generated and accumulated over the past decade. Each of the authors has had extensive experience in the field, and the expertise of the author team covers all branches of the discipline. We hope that both you and your students benefit from using this book and we welcome any suggestions that you have for future editions.

USING THIS MANUAL

This manual and the accompanying supplement to the text, *Readings in Management Accounting*, by S. Mark Young are designed to provide the instructor with the following:

- **Chapter reviews and outlines.** Each chapter begins with a chapter overview and proceeds with a chapter outline. Specific comments and teaching tips on the material are highlighted in boxes that are designated with the symbol: ▰▰▶▰.

- **Demonstration exercises/chapter review quizzes with solutions.** Each chapter contains a ten-question multiple choice quiz keyed into the learning objectives of each chapter. Solutions are provided at the end of the chapter review.

- **Articles to use to supplement the readings.** Unique to the ABKY text, state-of-the-art articles from a wide variety of sources contained in the text supplement, *Readings in Management Accounting,* are integrated into the *Instructor's Manual.* The Readings Book poses questions for students on each article and suggested answers in outline form also are provided in the Manual. While each instructor may want to ask his or her own questions, and will probably want to emphasize certain points within each article, the questions are included as a starting point.

  Note that readings are introduced in the body of the Manual via the symbol ▯. However, a synopsis of each article is contained at the end of each chapter so that the flow of the chapter outline is not too disrupted. This synopsis is identical to the one at the beginning of each section of *Readings in Management Accounting* as is included for the instructor's convenience. Also note that when using *Readings in Management Accounting* some of the readings may be used to supplement several different chapters as some articles often cover a few related topics.

- **Suggested cases to use to supplement the text.** In addition, to the readings, Harvard Business School Press cases as well as those from W. Rotch, B. Allen and C. Smith's *Cases in Management Accounting and Control Systems* (Prentice Hall, 1990) are suggested at the end of each chapter and are designated with the people symbol .

- A separate video supplement produced by Gerald Meyers also will be available to accompany the text.

As a closing note, since I believe strongly in continuous improvement please send or FAX me any suggestions that you have as to how the *Instructor's Manual* and *Readings in Management Accounting* can be improved. In particular, if you have readings that you think would add to the Readings Book please send them to me. I will be sure to acknowledge any contribution in the next edition. Thank you. I can be reached at any of the following addresses or numbers:

FAX at U.S.C.:   (213) 740-4848
Phone at U.S.C.:   (213) 747-2815
E-MAIL at U.S.C.:   MYOUNG@SBA.USC.EDU

S. Mark Young
School of Accounting
University of Southern California

INTERNET MAILING LISTS

Prentice Hall is proud to announce an important new free service pioneered by the ABKY author team. Tony Atkinson has set up an Internet list through which he will distribute important and timely pieces of information for management accounting professors to use in the classroom. This information will include summaries of articles from the popular press as well as abstracts from the academic literature, and will provide suggestions on how to make this information come alive in the classroom. Adopters will receive updates on the text and problem material in addition to valuable tips on how to best use the various ancillary materials that accompany the text.

Communication through the Internet will be two-sided: Adopters will be able to pose queries to any of out four authors and (with Professor Atkinson's help) distribute helpful suggestions of their own to other subscribers. It is our hope and expectation that this Internet list will become a lively forum for the exchange of information regarding the teaching of management accounting.

In order to demonstrate the kind of information adopters of ABKY will receive, we will make this service available to anyone teaching management accounting from now through June 1, 1995. You may gain access to this service by following these instructions. Address your Internet message to:

listserver@watarts.uwaterloo.ca

There is no need to include a subject for your message. Skip to the body of your message and type:

subscribe abkyd-L your name

Within a few days, you will receive a confirmation of your subscription. From that point on, you will receive regular information from Tony Atkinson.

We hope you'll give this valuable service a try. If you need additional information about Management Accounting or its teaching package, please contact your local Prentice Hall sales representative or call our toll-free Accounting and Taxation Hotline at (800) 227-1816.

Acknowledgements

I would like to thank Diane deCastro for all of her editorial assistance and support and Bill Webber for his encouragement on this project.

Chapter 1

Management Accounting:
Information That Creates Value

> ## CENTRAL FOCUS AND LEARNING OBJECTIVES
>
> This chapter provides a comprehensive overview of the field of management accounting. The chapter's learning objectives are to discuss:
>
> 1. The role for management accounting information in organizations
>
> 2. The differences between management accounting and financial accounting
>
> 3. Career opportunities for those who study management accounting
>
> 4. The different demands for management accounting information includes both financial and nonfinancial information
>
> 5. Historical and contemporary views of how management accounting creates value for organizations; its relation to operations, marketing and strategy
>
> 6. The role for management accounting in service organizations
>
> 7. The importance of understanding activities as the primary focus for measuring and managing performance

Chapter Overview

Chapter 1 presents an overview of the roles of management accounting information in organizations. Many different types of financial and non-financial management accounting information are required by people performing different tasks at various levels in the organization. The distinction between managerial and financial information is discussed.

A brief history of management accounting is provided, and how various developments have influenced operations, marketing and corporate strategy. The differences between manufacturing and service organizations are presented as well as the types of information that both require.

Finally, since activities are the basis for measurement and performance evaluation in a management accounting system both activity-based costing and activity-based management and their implications are discussed.

Chapter Outline _____

 Stress to students that this chapter introduces many important terms and concepts which form the foundation for an understanding of the rest of the book.

Learning Objective 1: The role of management accounting information in organizations. DO MULTIPLE CHOICE QUESTION 1.

I.   The Role of Management Accounting in Organizations

A.   A **management accounting system** is an information system that collects operational and financial data, processes it, stores it, and reports it to users such as workers, engineers, managers, executives).

B.   **Management accounting information** is output from a management accounting system (e.g., cost of a product, an activity, or a department).

C.   **Management accounting** is the process of producing financial and operating information regarding the economic condition of the organization for users internal to the organization such as employees and managers. The process should be driven by the informational needs of individuals internal to the organization, and should guide their operating and investment decisions.

Readings in Management Accounting

A very good reading to start the class is Reading 1.1, "Be Data Literate - Know What to Know," by Peter Drucker.

Learning Objective 2: The differences between management and financial accounting. DO MULTIPLE CHOICE QUESTION 2. See Exhibit 1-1.

D. In contrast, **financial accounting** differs from management accounting information as financial accounting information and financial statements are produced for external constituencies, such as shareholders, creditors, and governmental authorities. This process is heavily constrained by standard setting, regulatory, and tax authorities, and the auditing requirements of independent accountants (contrast with management accounting).

Learning Objective 3: Career opportunities for those who study management accounting. DO MULTIPLE CHOICE QUESTION 3.

E. Many types of individuals will benefit in their careers from an understanding of management accounting including: management accountants, scientists, engineers, many different types of general and staff managers.

Learning Objective 4: The different demands for management accounting information for different people in the organization. DO MULTIPLE CHOICE QUESTION 4. Note that the types of management accounting information will differ depending on the level of the organization.

Learning Objective 5: The reasons that management accounting information includes both financial and nonfinancial information. DO MULTIPLE CHOICE QUESTION 5.

II. Diversity of Management Accounting Information

There are many types of management accounting information and many uses. Examples include the quality of a service, quantitative inputs such as labor cost, profitability, efficiency and capacity use.

A. **Strategic information** guides the long-term decision-making of the organization. Strategic information can include the profitability of products, services, and customers; competitor's behavior; customer's preferences and trends; market opportunities and threats; and technological innovations.

1.   **Critical success factors** are factors such as quality, on-time delivery, cost reduction, customer service, or product performance, that create long term-profitability for the organization.

2.   **Benchmarking** is studying how other best-performing organizations, either internal or external to the firm, perform similar activities and processes.

 Students should be made aware of the many roles that management accounting information plays in an organization. Emphasize that all kinds of organizations such as hospitals, banks, insurance companies and others all use management accounting information, and that its role is becoming even more expansive than in the past.

B.   Functions of Management Accounting Information

1.   **Operational control** is the process of providing feedback to employees and their managers about the efficiency of activities being performed.

2.   **Product costing** is the process of measuring and assigning the costs of activities performed to design and produce individual products (and services, for non-manufacturing companies).

3.   **Customer costing** is the process of assigning marketing, selling, distribution, and administrative costs to individual customers so that the cost of serving each customer can be calculated.

4.   **Management control** is the process of providing information about the performance of managers and operating units.

Readings in Management Accounting

A good follow up to Drucker is, Reading 1.2, "What Production Managers Really Need to Know... Management Accountants Are Failing to Tell Them, by S. McKinnon and W. Bruns.

Learning Objective 6: Historical and contemporary views of how management accounting creates value for organizations: its relations to operations, marketing, and strategy. DO MULTIPLE CHOICE QUESTIONS 6 AND 7.

Readings in Management Accounting

Reading 1.3, Business Week's, "The Productivity Paradox," and "How the New Math of Productivity Adds Up," are particularly good readings to discuss at this point.

III.   Twentieth-Century Developments in Management Control.   A number of major innovations in management accounting occurred during the early part of the 20th century.

    A.   At the Dupont Corporation these included:

        1.   An **operating budget** which is a document that forecasts revenues and expenses during the next operating period, typically a year. The operating budget also authorizes spending on discretionary activities, such as research and development, advertising, maintenance and employee training.

        2.   The **capital budget** which is the management document that authorizes spending for resources, such as plant and equipment, that will have multiyear useful lifetimes.

        3.   **Return on investment** which is the calculation that relates the profitability of an organizational unit to the investment required to generate that

profitability. Often written as the return-on-sales multiplied by the ratio of sales to assets (or investment) employed.

ROI = Operating Income/Investment

= Operating Income/Sales x Sales/Investment

B. At General Motors these included concepts such as:

1. **Decentralized responsibility** which allows local division managers to make decisions on pricing, product mix, customer relationships, resource acquisition, materials sourcing, and operating processes without having to seek approval from higher-level managers. Decentralized responsibility also lets local managers make use of their superior access to information about local opportunities and threats.

2. **Centralized control** is the management process by which senior executives receive periodic information about decentralized divisional operations to assure that division managers are making decisions and taking actions that contribute to overall corporate goals.

3. A **flexible budget** is a forecast of what expenses should have been given the actual volume and mix of production and sales.

Learning Objective 7: The role for management accounting in service organizations. DO MULTIPLE CHOICE QUESTION 8. I would ask a student to pick manufacturing and service firms with which they are familiar and have him or her go down the list below contrasting the two on the various dimensions.

IV. Differences Between Service and Manufacturing Organizations

Service organizations:

A. Generally do not produce a product.

B. Have less direct contact with customers, so must be very sensitive to timeliness and quality of service.

C. Have no inventory, per se.

D. Quality is very hard to control in advance and thus defects are more likely and the consequences of poor service can be very strong.

Learning Objective 8: The importance of understanding activities as the primary focus for measuring performance. DO MULTIPLE CHOICE QUESTIONS 9 AND 10.

 This book really does represent a full integration of old and new concepts. Our goal has been to set the stage in this chapter to introduce many new concepts. As you introduce this last section to students you may wish to point out how quickly the world business environment has changed and how management accounting's role has changed as well. Point out that activity-based costing represents one of these major changes.

V. The Changing Competitive Environment

A. **Activity-based costing** is a procedure that measures the costs of objects such as products, services, and customers. Activity-based costing (ABC) first assigns resource costs to the activities performed by the organization. Then activity costs are assigned to products, customers, and services that benefit from or are creating the demand for activities.

B. **Activity-based management** is the management process that uses the information provided by an activity-based cost analysis to improve organizational profitability. Activity-based management (ABM) includes performing activities more efficiently, eliminating the need to perform certain activities that do not add value for customers, improving the design of products, and developing better relationships with customers and suppliers. The goal of

ABM is to enable customer needs to be satisfied while making fewer demands on organizational resources.

C. **Continuous improvement** is the ongoing process by which employees continually problem-solve and search for methods to reduce and eliminate waste, improve quality and reduce defects, shorten response and cycle times, and design products that are simpler to manufacture, deliver, and service.

D. **Employee empowerment** is allowing employees who are closest to operating processes, customers, and suppliers to make decisions. Employees are encouraged to solve problems and devise creative new approaches for performing work and satisfying customers.

E. **Total quality** is a management philosophy that attempts to eliminate all defects, waste, and activities that do not add value to customers; also refers to an organizational commitment to customer satisfaction.

Chapter Quiz/Demonstration Exercises_____

1. Management accounting information is developed for all of the following constituents EXCEPT:

   (a) workers
   (b) bondholders
   (c) managers
   (d) executives.

2. Management accounting has the following characteristics EXCEPT:

   (a) current, future oriented.
   (b) not regulated by the government.
   (c) disaggregate.
   (d) auditable.

3. Knowledge of management accounting has become important to a broad array of employees because:

   (a) the FASB has mandated it
   (b) the SEC has mandated it.
   (c) changes in the environment for all segments of business have led to an expansive role for such information.
   (d) auditors understand its importance and have pushed for an expansive role.

4. Management accounting information serves all of the following functions EXCEPT:

   (a) critical costing.
   (b) customer costing.
   (c) management control.
   (d) operational control.

5. Management accounting includes all of the following types of financial and nonfinancial information except:

   (a) unit product cost.
   (b) audited financial information.
   (c) profitability information.
   (d) quality information.

6. The return-on-investment ratio is:

(a) sales/operating income.
(b) operating income/sales.
(c) investment/sales.
(d) operating income/investment.

7. In the 1920's, General Motors CEO, Donaldson Brown, described the company's guiding philosophy as:

(a) centralized control with decentralized responsibility.
(b) decentralized control with centralized responsibility.
(c) centralized responsibility with decentralized control.
(d) decentralized authority with centralized responsibility.

8. The role for management accounting in service organizations in the 1990's has:

(a) decreased.
(b) stayed about the same.
(c) increased.
(d) no bearing whatsoever.

9. Activity based costing:

(a) encourages arbitrary cost allocations.
(b) assigns resource costs to activities, then activity costs are assigned to products.
(c) does not take organizational resources into account.
(d) assigns activity costs to resources, then resource costs to products.

10. In a total quality environment:

(a) quality problems are ignored as they will be corrected later by someone else.
(b) operators become problem solvers.
(c) quality assurance inspectors are constantly monitoring what employees do.
(d) operators look to quality assurance to solve problems.

Solutions to Chapter Quiz/Demonstration Exercises_____

Multiple Choice

1. b.
2. d.
3. c.
4. a.
5. b.
6. d.
7. a.
8. c.
9. b.
10. b.

SYNOPSIS OF *READINGS IN MANAGEMENT ACCOUNTING* AND QUESTIONS TO ASSIGN WITH SUGGESTED ANSWERS

Synopsis of Readings in Management Accounting

The readings in Chapter One all emphasize the changing role of management accounting information in today's business organizations. The first article (Reading 1.1) is Peter Drucker's, *"Be Data Literate - Know What to Know."* Drucker's article argues that there are three informational challenges facing executives. The first is to become information literate to know what information they need, when and in what form. The second challenge is how to obtain, test and combine information and integrate it into the existing information system. The final challenge, which is central to the study of management accounting, is that the data processing and accounting systems need to be brought together to decrease redundancy and increase compatibility. Drucker discusses the many new roles for accounting information and states: "Accounting has become the most intellectually challenging area in the field of management, and the most turbulent one."

The second article *"What Production Managers Really Want to Know. . .Management Accountants Are Failing to Tell Them,"* by Shannon McKinnon and William Bruns (Reading 1.2) continues with the theme established by Drucker that management accounting information can be highly relevant to any modern organization, but it must be responsive to specific user needs. McKinnon and Bruns conducted in-depth surveys of 73 top managers in production, sales, marketing, general management, and information systems in 12 firms in the U.S. and Canada. An interesting finding from this research is that production managers tend to make more use of physical unit data than dollar or financial data in the daily control of their operations, although financial measures play a central role in decision making over longer time periods. The article reports that many managers surveyed have developed their own information networks due to the inadequacies of many current accounting systems. To remedy this situation, they suggest that management accountants expand their role to include providing managers with more physical unit data, facilitating more information flows between sales and production and taking the lead to further integrate their organization's information system.

Synopsis of Readings in Management Accounting

The third article (Reading 1.3), divided into two parts, *"The Productivity Paradox,"* and the accompanying *"How the New Math of Productivity Adds Up,"* comes from a special report by **Business Week**. This article provides background regarding the changes that management accounting has been going through over the past decade. At the time the article was written, the United States was lagging behind Japan, Britain and France in productivity growth, despite huge investments in technology. One of the potential reasons cited for the lack of progress was out-moded management accounting systems that did not adequately provide appropriate information for investment justification or product costing. The article also discusses the role of CAM-I, Computer Integrated Manufacturing - International (now called the Consortium for Advanced Manufacturing -International) and the leading role it took to help bring practitioners, academics and government employees and agencies together to alter the way management accounting was being practiced. The article describes numerous problems with existing management accounting systems, many of which persist today.

Points to Include in Answering Questions from the Readings

1. What does Drucker mean when he says: "be data literate?"

   Student answers should include:
   a. What information do I need to make decisions.
   b. How do I obtain the information and how do I combine the information with existing information to make a good decision.
   c. How do I bring existing data bases and accounting systems together to reduce redundancy and improve compatibility so that I can make good decisions.

2. According to McKinnon and Bruns, what should management accountants do to provide better information?

   Student answers should include:
   a. Management accountants should help provide physical unit data to managers.
   b. Management accountants should play more of a role in facilitating interdepartmental communication across the different parts of the organization.
   c. Management accountants should redefine their roles to include management of information systems development and implementation.

3. What is meant by the term "productivity paradox," and what is a possible reason for the paradox?

   Student answers should include:
   a. The productivity paradox is that despite large investments in technology including automation, at the time of the article, the U.S. still lagged behind other competitors in many leading indicators.

   b. One reason for the paradox may be the inability of the cost and management accounting system to provide appropriate information on which to base decisions.

   c. Changes are needed in management accounting systems such as new measures for manufacturing performance relating to investment justification, quality and product costing.

Recommended Cases

For this opening chapter, no particular cases are recommended. However, the instructor could choose to spend some additional time discussing the material on history and how management accounting practice has changed over the past 10 years. Johnson and Kaplan's book *Relevance Lost: The Rise and Fall of Management Accounting* (Harvard Business School Press, 1987), will provide more background information to motivate such a discussion.

Chapter 2

Managing Activities

CENTRAL FOCUS AND LEARNING OBJECTIVES

This chapter presents material that illustrates the central role of activities and the linkages to management accounting, including:

1. The organization, its components, purpose, and major stakeholders

2. The idea of the organization as a sequence of activities in a value chain

3. The role of the customer in defining the focus of the activities in the value chain and the nature of value-added and nonvalue-added activities

4. The role of performance measures in helping organization members to manage the value chain

5. Benchmarking and continuous improvements as tools to improve organization performance

6. The relationship between organization activities and costs

7. The concept of just-in-time as a means to improve organization performance

Chapter Overview _____

Chapter 2 provides an introduction to the purpose and stakeholders of an organization. One of the key ideas introduced is the concept of the value chain. The value chain is composed of organizational activities. The customer perspective is critical in evaluating activities along the value chain as the outcomes associated with it ultimately reside with the customer. Four types of activities are discussed, input, processing, output and administrative.

This chapter also introduces the idea of critical success factors and critical performance indicators. The three most important critical success factors are service, quality and cost. Once each of these three factors is conceptualized by the firm, associated performance indicators must be developed to gauge success. In today's business climate, performance indicators have to be designed with continuous improvement in mind and often with the help of benchmarking what others are doing.

The linkages between activities and costs also are presented in the chapter, and the concepts of value and nonvalue-added, and efficient and effective activities are outlined. Variables related to improving performance and competitiveness such as cycle time and choices of facilities layout are discussed. Finally, the just-in-time manufacturing philosophy is presented as one way to avoid many of the costs and service problems associated with conventional thinking and facilities layouts.

Chapter Outline _____

> As you go through this chapter focus students on the links among the value chain concept, managing activities and the links to critical success factors and critical performance indicators.

Learning Objective 1: The organization, its components, purpose, and major stakeholders. DO MULTIPLE CHOICE QUESTION 1

I.   What is an organization's purpose and who are its stakeholders?

    A.   **Objectives** are the broad purposes of an organization or process. Objectives reflect the stakeholder requirements that the organization is committed to achieving, such as employee safety, profitability, and customer satisfaction.

    B.   **Stakeholders** are groups of people who have a legitimate claim on having an organization's objectives reflect their requirements. Each contributes to the organization and wants something in return. Stakeholders include:

        1.   Employees
        2.   Partners
        3.   Owners
        4.   The community
        5.   Customers

> *Go over Exhibit 2-2 to illustrate the contributions and requirements of the organization's stakeholders.*

Learning Objective 2: The idea of the organization as a sequence of activities in a value chain. DO MULTIPLE CHOICE QUESTION 2.

Learning Objective 3: The role of the customer in defining the focus of the activities in the value chain and the nature of value-added and nonvalue-added activities. DO MULTIPLE CHOICE QUESTIONS 3 AND 4.

Readings in Management Accounting

Reading 2.1, J. Shank and V. Govindarajan's "Strategic Cost Management and the Value Chain," links management accounting and the value chain concept. Reading 2.2, M. Ostenga's "Activities: The Focal Point of Total Cost Management," stresses the key role of activities.

II.   The Organization as a Sequence of Activities or Value Chain

   A.   A **value chain** is a sequence of activities whose objective is to provide a product to a customer or provide an intermediate good or service in a larger value chain. *Each step in the value chain should add something that the **customer values** in the product or service.*

   B.   An **activity** is a unit of work, or task, with a specific goal. Examples of activities are processing an insurance claim, waiting on a customer in a restaurant, and welding two components together. There are four broad categories of activities:

      1.   **Input activities** - those relating to getting ready to make a product or deliver a service.

2. **Processing activities** - those related to producing the product or service.

3. **Output activities** - those related to dealing with a customer.

4. **Administrative activities** - those that support 1-3, including, human resources, and general administration.

C. Process Measurement and Improvement

1. The role for employees is to manage the activities in the value chain in an effective and efficient manner.

   a. The organization, is **effective** if meets its objectives.

   b. An organization is **efficient** if it achieves its objectives using the fewest possible resources.

2. Four steps can be used to determine the level of effectiveness and efficiency of activities:

   a. **Identify** and depict the activities in the value chain. **Charting** is a term that is used to visually depict each activity.
   b. **Measure** the performance of each activity.
   c. **Analyze** the performance measures and the way that activities are being undertaken.
   d. **Improve** the performance of activities, given c, above. An **activity improvement** is making the performance of an activity better in terms of the organization's objectives.

Learning Objective 4: The role of performance measures in helping organization members to manage the value chain. DO MULTIPLE CHOICE QUESTIONS 5 AND 6.

III. Performance Measures and Performance Measurement and Performance Standards

A. **Critical performance indicators** are performance measures used to assess an organization's performance on its critical success factors.

B. **Critical success factors** are elements of performance required for an organization's success. Three of these related to the ability of the organization to meet customer requirements are:

1. **Service** consists of the product's tangible and intangible features promised to the customer. Also known as value in use.

2. **Quality** is the difference between the promised and the realized level of service

3. **Cost** is efficiency to the provider of a product, that is, using minimum resources to achieve objectives, or the price paid to the purchaser of a product.

 Review Exhibit 2-4 to see the linkage between critical success factors and critical performance indicators. Be sure that students understand the relationship between the two.

C. Performance Measurement

1. An effective system of performance measurement includes critical performance indicators that:

a. consider each activity from the **customer's perspective.**
b. evaluates each activity using **customer-validated measures of performance.**

i. An **output** is a physical measure of production or activity, such as the number of units produced or the amount of time spent doing something.

        ii.   **An outcome** is the value attributed to output by the customer, for example, the number of good units of production and the amount of client satisfaction generated by a service.

    c.   is **comprehensive** in considering all facets of activity performance for customers.

    d.   provides **feedback** to organizational employees on how to identify problems and improve.

        i.   A **signal** is information provided to a decision maker. There are two types of signals: (1) a warning that there is a problem and (2) a diagnostic that identifies the problem.

D.   **Control** is the set of methods and tools that organization members use to keep the organization on track toward achieving its objectives.

> Learning Objective 5: Benchmarking and continuous improvements as tools to improve organization performance. DO MULTIPLE CHOICE QUESTIONS 7 AND 8. Benchmarking will be discussed again later in Chapter 14.

E.   Performance standards

    1.   **Continuous improvement** is the relentless search to:

        a.   document, understand, and improve the activities that the organization undertakes to meet its customers' requirements.

        b.   eliminate nonvalue-added activities.

        c.   improve the performance of value-added activities.

    2.   **Cooperative Benchmarking** is an organization's search for, and implementation of, the best way to do something as practiced by another organization.

3. **Deming Wheel** is a means to organize process improvements, which involves a continuous cycle of planning, doing, checking, and action.

 Review Exhibit 2-5 on the Deming Wheel.

Learning Objective 6: The relationship between organization activities and costs. DO MULTIPLE CHOICE QUESTION 9.

IV. Organization Activities and Costs

    A. Managing by the numbers is a process of using cost information to make decisions but it has several problems:

        1. It is ineffective.
        2. It assumes that cost is the only relevant measure of an activity's performance.
        3. It does not recognize the reasons that costs exist.

    B. A more effective method of cost control involves understanding what causes costs and what activities add value.

        1. **A Value-added activity** is one that, if eliminated, would reduce the product's service to the customer.

        2. **Non-value added activity** is an activity that presents the opportunity for cost reduction without reducing the product's service potential to the customer.

    C. **Activity analysis** is an approach to operations control that involves the application of steps of continuous improvement to an activity - also known as value analysis. Four steps are involved:

        a. **Identify** process objectives.
        b. **Record** the activities used to complete a product or service from beginning to end by charting. **Storyboarding** is an example of charting.

c. **Classify** all activities as value and non-value added.

d. **Continuously improve** the efficiency of all activities.

V. Time Requirements for Activities and Cycle Time

A. **Cycle time** is the total time the organization needs to complete an activity or a process. There are four types of activities which when summed together give total cycle time. As non-value added activities related to these decrease cycle time will decrease as will costs. The four types are:

1. Processing
2. Moving
3. Storing (waiting)
4. Inspecting

B. **Manufacturing cycle efficiency** is the ratio of the time required by value-added activities in a value chain to the total time required by all activities in the value chain.

Manufacturing cycle efficiency =

Processing time/(Processing time + Moving time + Storing time + Inspection time)

C. There are three general types of **facilities layout** that can affect the level of inventories and inventory-related costs. Management accountants are very concerned with inventory levels as the cost of holding inventory are very high. These are:

1. **Process layout** is a means of organizing a production activity so that all similar equipment or functions are grouped together, for example, a university where faculty are housed by department.

2. **Product layout** is a means of organizing a production activity so that equipment or functions are organized to make a specific product, for example, an automobile assembly line.

3.   **Cell manufacturing** is a means of organizing a production activity so that all the equipment needed to make a good or service is grouped together.

Learning Objective 7: The concept of just-in-time as a means to improve organization performance. DO MULTIPLE CHOICE QUESTION 10.

Readings in Management Accounting

G. Foster and C. Horngren's "Cost Accounting and Cost Management in a JIT Environment," Reading 2.3 illustrates a number of management accounting issues related to JIT.

E.   **Just-in-time or JIT** is making a good or service only when the customer, who may be internal or external, requires it. This philosophy is based on the elimination of all nonvalue-added activities to reduce cost and time. JIT helps avoid many of the costs and service problems associated with conventional manufacturing and facilities layout, and management accounting:

1.   must support the move to JIT by monitoring, identifying and communicating to decision makers the sources of delay, error and waste in the system.

2.   is simplified by JIT as there are fewer inventories to monitor and record.

When reviewing this material, *note the strong ties between management accounting and operations management. Throughout the textbook other links related to strategy and organizational behavior will be made.*

Chapter Quiz/Demonstration Exercises _____

1.   Partners in an organization contribute:

    (a)   effort and skills
    (b)   capital
    (c)   the surrounding environment
    (d)   goods, services and information

2.   Each of the following is a processing activity in the value chain, EXCEPT:

    (a)   operating machines to produce the product
    (b)   moving work-in-process
    (c)   billing the customer
    (d)   inspecting partially completed products

3.   Whose is the dominant perspective in valuing activities in the value chain?

    (a)   each employee's
    (b)   the customer's
    (c)   the owner's
    (d)   the board of director's

4.   Effectiveness is achieved if the organization:

    (a)   achieves its objectives
    (b)   is improving its performance
    (c)   it uses the fewest resources possible to achieve its objectives.
    (d)   uses benchmarking to compare themselves to others

5.   Each of the following is one of the three broad critical success factors to meet customer requirements, EXCEPT:

    (a)   cost
    (b)   quality
    (c)   feedback
    (d)   service

6. The critical difference between outcome and output measurement is that:

   (a) output focuses on effectiveness in meeting customer requirements but outcome does not.
   (b) outcome focuses on efficiency in meeting customer requirements but output does not.
   (c) output focuses on efficiency in meeting customer requirements but outcome does not.
   (d) outcome focuses on effectiveness in meeting customer requirements but output does not.

7. The Deming Wheel involves the following steps, EXCEPT:

   (a) Planning
   (b) Doing
   (c) Action
   (d) Redesign

8. The _____ Company is credited with developing the systematic approach to benchmarking that many organizations use today.

   (a) Chrysler
   (b) Xerox
   (c) Toyota
   (d) Manville

9. The key driver of costs are:

   (a) activities
   (b) plant
   (c) employees
   (d) computer technology

10. Critical performance indicators for JIT systems consist of the following, EXCEPT:

    (a) inventory levels
    (b) number of failures
    (c) number of customer orders per month
    (d) amount of moving

Solutions to Chapter Quiz/Demonstration Exercises _____

1.   d
2.   c
3.   b
4.   a
5.   c
6.   d
7.   b
8   b
9.   a
10.   c

SYNOPSIS OF *READINGS IN MANAGEMENT ACCOUNTING* AND QUESTIONS TO ASSIGN WITH SUGGESTED ANSWERS

Synopsis of Readings in Management Accounting

John Shank and Vijay Govindarajan's article, "*Strategic Cost Management and the Value Chain*," (Reading 2.1) begins the series of articles related to Chapter Two. One key distinction the authors draw is between the value-added and value chain concepts. The value-added concept is the one typically adopted by traditional management accounting and has a focus that is strictly internal to the firm. The central idea is to maximize the difference between the purchase price of raw materials and selling price of products (or the value-added). This view states that this is the only area in which an organization can influence costs. The value chain concept takes a much more expansive approach viewing each organization as only one link in a chain that begins with basic raw materials and ends when the customer retires the product. Within this framework each part of the chain is broken down into strategically relevant activities and analyzed accordingly. The article uses a case study of the paper industry to illustrate its arguments.

Michael Ostrenga's article, "*Activities: The Focal Point of Total Cost Management*," (Reading 2.2) focuses on the concept of total cost management (TCM). TCM is a philosophy of managing all organizational resources as well as the activities that consume these resources. Based on his experience as a consultant with Ernst and Young Ostrenga, discusses the key underlying components of TCM including process-value analysis, activity-based process costing, activity-based product costing, responsibility accounting, and performance and investment management. The article details the role of each of these components and illustrates the central role of managing activities.

Synopsis of Readings in Management Accounting

Based on discussions with many managers who have adopted the just-in-time manufacturing philosophy and method, George Foster and Charles Horngren's article, *"Cost Accounting and Cost Management in a JIT Environment,"* (Reading 2.3) raises a number of issues relating to how management accounting must change to accommodate the use of JIT. Since JIT changes many of the activities that underlie the manufacturing process, management accounting systems have to change in order to provide relevant information for decision-making. For example, JIT can greatly reduce or eliminate the traditional purchasing function, change the flow of production activities, and increase the direct traceability of many indirect costs. If a traditional management accounting system is used with JIT, many of the benefits of the system will be lost. For more background on the behavioral and organizational issues relating to JIT and other Japanese manufacturing practices, a related reading from Chapter Fourteen (Reading 14.4), Mark Young's *"A Framework for Successful Adoption and Performance of Japanese Manufacturing Practices in the United States,"* is recommended.

Points to Include in Answering Questions from the Readings

1.   What are structural and executional cost drivers and how are they distinguished in Shank and Govindarajan's article?

Student answers should include:
a.   Structural cost drivers come from an organization's choices about its underlying economic structure. These include
        i.   scale - the size of investment
        ii.   scope - the degree of vertical integration
        iii.   experience - how often the organization has done what it is doing
        iv.   technology - the process technologies are used
        v.   complexity - the number of products or services offered.
b.   Executional cost drivers are those factors that allow organizations to perform its tasks successfully. These include:
        i.   workforce involvement - level of commitment
        ii.   total quality management - commitment to quality
        iii.   capacity utilization - scale choices of plant
        iv.   plant layout - how efficiently is plant organized
        v.   product configuration - effectiveness of product design
        vi.   linkages with suppliers or customers - the level of linkages given the value chain analysis.

Points to Include in Answering Questions from the Readings

2.   Describe the four major steps of process value analysis (PVA) in Ostrenga's article. Is each of them necessary?

Student answers should include:
a.   Process Definition: documents flow, identification of internal and external customer's needs, definition of outputs of each step, etc.
b.   Activity Analysis: define activities within each process, identify value added and nonvalue added customer requirements, determine cycle time of each activity, etc.
c.   Driver Analysis: develop cause and effect driver identification, perform Pareto analysis on the drivers and activities they control.
d.   Opportunity Improvement Planning: develop perspective charts on value added and non value added, develop opportunity improvement plan, etc.

3.   For firms adopting JIT production, what major changes in management accounting systems are being made?

Student answers should include:
a.   Direct traceability of costs are increased.
b.   Cost pools for indirect activities are being reduced.
c.   Emphasis on individual labor and overhead variances are being reduced.
d.   The level of detailed information recorded on work tickets is being reduced.
e.   All of the above will result in a very different, more effective management accounting system.

Recommended Cases and Materials

1. A very introductory case is "Breezy Boat Company," in the Rotch et al. Case book. The case asks students to think of the types of activities and decisions related to the company and the types of management accounting information that is needed.

2. A much more advanced case, "Tektronix: Portable Instruments Division" cases (A) and (B) can be assigned to correspond with the material on JIT and the Horngren and Foster article. (Harvard Business School Cases 188-142 (case A) and 188-143 (case B); Teaching Note: 5-191-189).

3. I would recommend reviewing Shank and Govindarajan's book, *Strategic Cost Management - The New Tool for Competitive Advantage* (Free Press, 1993) for more background on strategic cost management.

4. For instructors who have not had a great deal of experience using the case method I recommend the following:

    a.   J. S. Hammond III, "Learning By the Case Method," Harvard Note 9-376-241.

    b.   C. R. Christensen, *Teaching and the Case Method* (Harvard #9-387-001) and teaching Guide (5-387-010).

Chapter 3

Cost Concepts

CENTRAL FOCUS AND LEARNING OBJECTIVES

This chapter outlines the fundamentals of costing and cost classification, including:

1. How costs are classified based on function

2. The difference between direct and indirect costs

3. How overhead costs arise

4. The difference between unit-related, batch-related, product-sustaining, and facility-sustaining activity cost drivers

5. How cost relations with activities and their drivers are expressed as equations

6. How information is collected to estimate activity costs

7. How cost concepts extend to service organizations

8. How standard costs are determined

9. Uses and limitations of standard cost systems

Chapter Overview

This chapter introduces a number of important definitions of the various types of costs. Traditional concepts of direct and indirect costs as well as how overhead costs arise are presented. One important feature is the description of the change in the way that we have thought about costing terminology.

The chapter illustrates the transition in thinking from the traditional approach to new concepts of classification such as unit-related, batch-related, product sustaining and facility-sustaining activity cost drivers.

Cost relations and activities also are expressed in a series of equations. Material is presented that discusses how information is collected to estimate activity costs. Other topics include how cost concepts extend to service organizations and the uses and limitations of standard costing.

Chapter Outline _____

 As you present this material, it may be useful to mention to students at several points how cost concepts have changed so much over the past 5 years in particular. This is also the time to present one major development in thinking about costing and that is the classification based on unit-related, batch-related, product sustaining and facility-sustaining costs.

Learning Objective 1: How costs are classified based on function. DO MULTIPLE CHOICE PROBLEMS 1 and 2.

I.   Functional Cost Classifications in Traditional Systems

     A.   Costs Versus Expenses

          1.   **Cost** is the monetary value of goods and services expended to obtain current or future benefits.

          2.   **Expenses** are either costs for which benefits were already derived in the current period (such as cost of goods sold), or costs whose benefits cannot be matched easily with the products or services of another period (such as advertising).

     B.   Product Versus Period Costs

          1.   **Product costs** are costs associated with the manufacture of products.

          2.   **Period costs** are costs treated as expenses in the period in which they are incurred because they cannot be associated with the manufacture of products.

3. **Production volume** is the overall measure, such as number of units, of various products manufactured in a given time period.

C. Manufacturing Versus Non-manufacturing Costs

1. **Manufacturing costs** are all costs of transforming raw materials into finished product. Traditionally only manufacturing costs are included when valuing finished goods inventory and only manufacturing costs are considered product costs.

2. **Nonmanufacturing costs** are all costs other than manufacturing costs. Traditionally, these costs are considered period costs and are expenses in the period in which they are incurred. These include:

   a. **Distribution costs**, which include costs of delivering finished products to customers.

   b. **Selling costs**, which includes sales personnel salaries and commissions and other sales office expenses.

   c. **Marketing costs**, which include advertising and publicity expenses.

   d. **Research and development costs**, which include expenditures for designing and bringing new products to market.

   e. **General and administrative costs** which include expenses such as CEO's salary and legal and general accounting costs and those that do not come under any of the other categories listed.

Learning Objective 2: The difference between direct and indirect costs. DO MULTIPLE CHOICE PROBLEM 3.

D.   Direct Versus Indirect Costs.

1.   **Direct costs** are those that can be traced easily to the product manufactured or service tendered. These costs are assigned to products directly based on the measured quantity of the *resources consumed* for their manufacture.   Examples are:

a.   **Direct materials cost** - the cost of all materials and parts that can be traced directly to the product.

b.   **Direct labor cost** - wages and fringe benefits paid to workers involved directly in manufacturing a product.

Review Equation 3.1

$$C = P * Q$$

C = cost of input resource
P = price per unit of resource
Q = quantity of resource

Readings in Management Accounting

Reading 3.1 by R. Cooper and R. Kaplan, "Activity-Based Systems: Measuring the Costs of Resource Usage," can be assigned at this point, The critical idea to impart is activity-based cost systems are different from traditional systems in that the emphasis on ABC systems is on resources consumed and not resources that are available for use. This article can be used at several other points in the book.

---

2.   **Indirect costs** are those that cannot be traced easily to products or services produced; also referred to as manufacturing overhead costs.

a. **Manufacturing costs** or burden are indirect costs of transforming raw materials into finished product; indirect manufacturing costs. Examples include:

    i. Wages and benefits paid to **production supervisors** who do not directly produce the product.

    ii. Wages and benefits paid to **other support personnel** who are involved with scheduling, moving materials, inspection, etc.

The rather dramatic decrease in direct labor cost as a percentage of total product cost in many of today's manufacturing organizations was a signal that much more attention needed to be paid to the increasing cost of overhead. Point out to students that we have known for a long time that the overhead allocation process was arbitrary, but the large increase in this account also was an impetus for management accountants and others to devise much more accurate resource/overhead allocation systems.

II. Cost Structure in Today's Environment

    A. The composition of manufacturing costs has changed in recent years. For instance, the proportion of direct labor in the early 1900s could have been as high as 50% of unit product cost. Today direct labor cost may be as small as 5% of unit product cost.

    B. Also, the proportion of overhead costs have increased, and thus, new cost systems are now paying much more attention to them.

III. Activity-Based Analysis of Costs

Learning Objective 3: How overhead costs arise. DO MULTIPLE CHOICE PROBLEM 4.

A.   Why are overhead costs incurred?

    1.   Manufacturing overhead costs are indirect costs of transforming raw materials into finished product.

    2.   Overhead costs increase with the volume of activities required to support production.

B.   Types of production activities.

Learning Objective 4: The difference between unit-related, batch-related, product-sustaining, and facility-sustaining activity cost drivers. DO MULTIPLE CHOICE PROBLEM 5.

Readings in Management Accounting

Robin Cooper's "Cost Classification in Unit-Based and Activity-Based Manufacturing Cost Systems," Reading 3.2 can be assigned to provide more background. The article introduces the typology of activities for activity-based costing.

An interesting and timely application of Cooper's typology is in Reading 3.3 by Jerry Kreuze and Gale Newell, "ABC and Life-Cycle Costing for Environmental Expenditures."

---

    1.   **Unit-related activities** are those whose levels are related to the number of units produced.

    2.   **Batch-related activities** are those whose levels are related to the number of batches produced.

    3.   **Product-sustaining activities** are those activities performed to support the production of individual products.

4. **Facility-sustaining activities** are those performed to provide the managerial infrastructure and to support the upkeep of the plant.

IV. Activity Cost Drivers

A. **Activity cost driver** is a unit of measurement for the level (or quantity) of the activity performed.

Learning Objective 5: How cost relations with activities and their drivers are expressed as equations. DO MULTIPLE CHOICE PROBLEM 6.

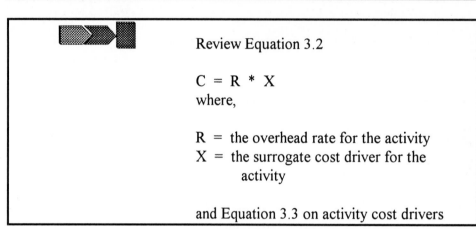

Review Equation 3.2

$C = R * X$
where,

R = the overhead rate for the activity
X = the surrogate cost driver for the activity

and Equation 3.3 on activity cost drivers

B **Activity overhead rate** is the ratio of the cost of resources to provide an activity to the level of the capacity made available by those resources.

Learning Objective 6: How information is collected to estimate activity costs. DO MULTIPLE CHOICE PROBLEM 7.

1. To determine the rates, first identify activity costs, select a cost driver measure and then determine the rates.

2. Note that the cost of activities depends on the available capacity of the driver rather than the actual use of the capacity.

Review Equations 3.4, 3.5 and 3.6 on multiple activities and cost distortion

Equation 3.5 for multiple activities:

$$C = C_1 + C_2 + C_3 + C_4 + C_5$$

$$= R_1 * X_1 + R_2 * X_2 + R_3 * X_3 + R_4 * X_4 + R_5 * X_5$$

Learning Objective 7: How cost concepts extend to service organizations. **DO MULTIPLE CHOICE PROBLEM 8.**

One exercise that you might try is to have students list 3 or 4 different types of services. Ask them to discuss what the output of the service is, whether it can be measured easily and how they would know if the service was effective.

V. Cost Concepts for Service Organizations

A. Services produced cannot be inventoried for future sale, thus, cost accounting systems associated with most service organizations do not have to worry about financial reporting requirements of inventory valuation.

B. Regulatory requirements for financial reporting for services often limits the structure of cost reports.

C. Output is difficult to measure as services produce less tangible and measurable product than manufacturing organizations.

D. **Operating overhead** is indirect costs of producing services in a service organization.

Learning Objective 8: How standard costs are determined. **DO MULTIPLE CHOICE PROBLEM 9.**

VI.   Standard Cost Accounting Systems

A.   **Standard costs** are efficient and attainable benchmarks established in advance for the costs of activity resources that should be consumed by each product. Standard cost systems are used for three main reasons:

1.   Estimate product costs.

2.   Budget for costs and expenditures.

3.   Control costs relative to standards.

a.   **Cost variances** arise when there are differences between standards and actual costs.

Learning Objective 9. Uses and limitations of standard cost systems. DO MULTIPLE CHOICE PROBLEM 10.

B.   Standards should be set at levels that are efficient and attainable.

C.   Standard costing systems are most useful when production technology is stable.

Readings in Management Accounting

Reading 3.4, Yasuhiro Monden and John Lee's article, "How A Japanese Auto Maker Reduces Costs," presents an alternative to standard costing known as Kaizen costing. This article should promote a lot of discussion. It can also be used later in Chapters 8 and 9.

Chapter Quiz/Demonstration Exercises _____

1. Costs and expenses are:

    (a) always the same thing.
    (b) never the same thing.
    (c) always treated the same for income statement purposes.
    (d) sometimes the same depending on the type of cost.

2. Period costs are:

    (a) treated as expenses in the period in which they are incurred.
    (b) always directly traceable to products.
    (c) costs including direct labor.
    (d) costs including manufacturing overhead.

3. Each of the statements below is true about indirect costs, EXCEPT:

    (a) they cannot be traced easily to products or services.
    (b) they are also referred to as overhead costs.
    (c) they are actually a subset of direct costs.
    (d) they are also referred to as burden.

4. Overhead costs have increased in today's manufacturing environment because:

    (a) managers have let them get out of control.
    (b) there is now a shift toward greater automation.
    (c) fewer direct materials are being used in production.
    (d) direct labor costs have increased.

5. Production activities are now classified into the following categories, EXCEPT:

    (a) unit-related.
    (b) batch-related.
    (c) period-sustaining.
    (d) facility-sustaining.

6. Cost of an input resource, C, can be expressed as:

    (a) $C = P * Q$, where P = price per unit of resource and Q = quantity of resource in units.

(b) $C = P + Q$, where P = price per unit of resource and Q = quantity of resource in units.

(c) $C = P/Q$, where P = price per unit of resource and Q = quantity of resource in units.

(d) $C = Q/P$, where P = price per unit of resource and Q = quantity of resource in units.

7.   Each of the following is an appropriate way to collect information to estimate activity costs, EXCEPT:

(a)   observing the organization in detail.
(b)   examining cost accounting records.
(c)   interviewing employees.
(d)   rely exclusively on past records.

8.   A key difference between service and manufacturing organizations is that:

(a)   in a service organization output is more tangible and measurable than in a manufacturing organization.
(b)   in a manufacturing organization output is less tangible and measurable than in a service organization.
(c)   in a service organization output is less tangible and measurable than in a manufacturing organization.
(d)   services produced can be inventoried much easier than manufactured products.

9.   Many firms use standard cost systems for the following reasons, EXCEPT:

(a)   they are used to estimate product costs.
(b)   they are much easier to develop than actual costs.
(c)   they help in budgeting for costs and expenditures.
(d)   they control costs relative to standards.

10.   A danger in over reliance on managing with standard cost accounting systems is:

(a)   costs are never really in control.
(b)   actual costs are never really considered.
(c)   actual costs play too big a role.
(d)   a mindset can be created of just simply trying to meet the standards.

Solutions to Chapter Quiz/Demonstration Exercises_____

1. d.
2. a.
3. c.
4. b.
5. c.
6. a.
7. d.
8. c.
9. b.
10. d.

SYNOPSIS OF *READINGS IN MANAGEMENT ACCOUNTING* AND QUESTIONS TO ASSIGN WITH SUGGESTED ANSWERS

Synopsis of Readings in Management Accounting

Robin Cooper and Robert Kaplan's "*Activity-Based Systems: Measuring the Costs of Resource Usage,*" (Reading 3.1) presents one of the key distinguishing ideas between traditional and activity-based costing systems. Traditional costing systems tend to use allocation bases such as direct labor and machine hours that are volume-driven. However, the resource demands of customers and products often are not proportional to the volume of units sold or produced. Thus, traditional systems do not accurately measure the costs of resources used to produce products; rather, they rely on the cost of resources supplied. Activity-based costing systems overcome this problem by focusing on the demands of resources needed to perform activities to produce outputs. The demands derive from variation in the diversity and complexity of products and customer mix.

The second reading (Reading 3.2), "*Cost Classification in Unit-Based and Activity-Based Manufacturing Cost Systems,*" by Robin Cooper, presents an important advance in the classification of activities in manufacturing processes. Based on an analysis of fifty costing systems representing thirty-one firms, Cooper classifies activities in unit-level, batch-level, product-level and facility-level activities. For unit-based activities, costs are assigned in strict proportion to production volume; batch level activities work under the assumption that inputs are consumed in direct proportion to the number of batches; product-level activities assume that inputs are consumed to sustain production of the variety of products that an organization produces, and facility-level activities those activities common to many products and whose allocation is done on an arbitrary basis. This classification of activities forms the basis of an activity-based costing system.

"*ABC and Life-Cycle Costing for Environmental Expenditures,*" by Jerry Kreuze and Gale Newell (Reading 3.3), presents an interesting application of ABC and Cooper's classification to environmental costing settings. The article addresses issues related to the costs of hazardous waste disposal, cleaning up polluted water, soil, and buildings, and many other issues. The concept of life-cycle costing also is introduced and

Synopsis of Readings in Management Accounting

is extremely pertinent for dealing with products or processes that may ultimately result in environmental problems. For instance, Kreuze and Newell state that responsibility for dealing with hazardous waste essentially lasts forever. The ABC classification of costs is used very effectively to illustrate how environmental costs can be separated and managed.

The last article for this chapter (Reading 3.4), Yosuhiro Monden and John Lee's, "*How A Japanese Auto Maker Reduces Costs,*" presents a challenge to traditional standard costing methods by introducing the concept of Kaizen costing. Kaizen costing is tied directly to continuous improvement and its goal is to reduce actual costs below the level of standard costs. The article illustrates Kaizen costing at Daihatsu Motor Company in Osaka, Japan. Using Kaizen costing, a target reduction rate is determined within the parameters of the profit planning process. One potential difficulty with the system is that it can be quite stressful for manufacturing personnel as cost targets keep getting lower and lower. Daihatsu uses a grace period to help reduce stress. Kaizen costing is used in addition to the standard costing system, and its strength is its tie to the overall profit planning process of the firm.

Points to Include in Answering Questions from the Readings

1. What important insights about resource usage come from activity-based costing systems in Cooper and Kaplan's article?

    Student answers should include:
    a. Traditional costing systems are based on volume-driven allocation bases that often do not measure accurately the costs of resources used in producing output.
    b. Activity-based costing systems estimate the resources used to produce products. They *do not* rely on the assumption that resources are demanded in proportion to the total volume of units produced or sold.
    c. Also, activity-based cost systems do not model how expenses or spending vary in the short-run. Instead ABC systems estimate the costs of resources used to perform activities needed to produce a variety of products.

2. What are the important elements of Cooper's definition of an ABC system?

    Student answers should include:
    a. An ABC identifies and classifies the major activities of an organization's manufacturing process into one of the following four categories:
        i.   unit-level
        ii.   batch-level
        iii. product-level
        iv.   facility-level
    b. Costs in categories i to iii can be assigned to products using the most appropriate cost drivers.
    c. The costs of facility-level activities can be treated as period costs or arbitrarily allocated to products.

Points to Include in Answering Questions from the Readings

3.   Describe the four levels of environmental costs that are important to a full costing analysis as discussed in the Kreuze and Newell article.

Student answers should include:
a.   Usual costs and operating costs - those associated with products such as materials, plant and equipment, etc.
b.   Hidden regulatory costs - costs of governmental and regulatory costs of compliance including notification, permitting, testing, training and inspection, etc.
c.   Contingent liability costs - includes penalties and fines for noncompliance and legal claims and settlements for personal injuries, etc.
d.   Less tangible costs - includes by becoming environmentally responsible by doing things such as reducing pollution or altering product designs for more environmental safety, cost savings (less tangible costs) can result.

4.   What are the strengths and weaknesses of Kaizen costing according to Monden and Lee?

Student answers should include:
a.   A strength is that Kaizen costing is much more aggressive at reducing costs than standard costing. Ultimately, this will make the user of the method more competitive.
b.   Another strength is that Kaizen costing is tied directly into profit planning for the firm.
c.   A weakness is the costs to employees who may become overly stressed as they have to constantly think of new ways to reduce costs.

Recommended Cases

1. An introductory case is "Englehardt Art Glass" in the Rotch, et al., Case Book.

2. Two more advanced case is "Bridgeton Industries" HBS Case 190-185 and the teaching note 5-191-168 on cost concepts and overhead rates, and "Paramount Cycle" HBS Case 180-069 and the teaching note 5-182-200.

3. A good case to complement the Cooper and Kaplan reading is HBS Case 9-191-067, Hewlett-Packard Queensferry Telecommunications Division 5-191-197.

4. A very advanced set of cases to use with Cooper's article are John Deere (A) and (B), HBS case numbers, 187-107 and 187-108 and the accompanying teaching notes, 9-187-107 and 9-187-108.

Chapter 4

Cost Behavior

> **CENTRAL FOCUS AND LEARNING OBJECTIVES**
>
> This chapter introduces the essential elements of cost behavior including:
>
> 1. The difference between fixed and variable costs
>
> 2. The ways in which the commitment and consumption of activity resources influence cost variability
>
> 3. The reasons why activity costs tend to be more variable in the long run
>
> 4. What the normal costs of an activity are
>
> 5. The ways to estimate overhead costs for multiple activities supporting the production of multiple products
>
> 6. Breakeven analysis
>
> 7. The way to sketch a planning model that captures the relationship between revenues, costs and production volumes

Chapter Overview _____

The differences between fixed, variable and mixed costs are presented in this chapter using a number of illustrations. Also included on this topic are a series of basic equations and graphs to aid in understanding the material.

Several topics from basic economics such as cost curves and economies and diseconomies are introduced as are the relevant range and step fixed and step variable costs. Building on Chapter 3, discussion also centers on the linkages among resource allocation, resource commitment and consumption of resources and how these variables influence cost variability. The section on normal costs is a departure from other texts and incorporates the ideas of available capacity.

Cost behavior is also introduced and tied in with a discussion of discretionary and committed resources. Much of the material in the chapter is also incorporated into a presentation of breakeven analysis. The chapter concludes with a planning model of revenues and expenses designed to maximize profits.

Note that the chapter begins in a fairly traditional manner and then new ideas related to commitment and consumption of activity resources and how they influence cost variability are introduced.

Learning Objective 1. The difference between fixed and variable costs. DO MULTIPLE CHOICE QUESTIONS 1 and 2.

I.   Cost Behavior and Production Volume

Managers are concerned with how costs change with changes in the level of one key cost driver which is the volume of production. Costs are classified based on their relation to changes in production volume.

A.   **Fixed costs** do not change with changes in the level of production over short periods of time. In other words, they are independent of the level of production

B.   **Variable costs** change in proportion to changes in production volume. They represent resources whose consumption can be adjusted to match the demand placed on them

 Review Exhibits 14- through 14-6 for examples

C.   **Mixed costs** are those comprised of both fixed and variable cost components

 Review Exhibits 14-7 and 14-8 for examples
Note Equation 4.1

Total costs = Fixed costs + (variable cost rate) *
                 quantity of production, or

$$C = F + VQ$$

Readings in Management Accounting

Reading 4.1, Robin Cooper and Robert Kaplan's "How Cost Accounting Distorts Product Costs can be assigned at this point. This is one of the very early articles that really motivated a great deal of discussion on traditional cost accounting.

     D.   Representing Activity Costs as Fixed or Variable

               Many unit-related measures are closely related to production volume. However, over a sufficiently long period of time when managers can adjust the level of resources for batch-related activities some batch-related measures also may vary with production volume. See Equations 4.2 and 4.3.

II.   Costs in an Economic Framework

     A.   A **cost curve** is a graph of costs plotted against activity cost driver or production volume. See Exhibit 4-9.

     B.   **Economies of scale** means decreasing average costs with increases in production volume

     C   **Capacity constraints** are limitations on the quantity that can be produced because the capacity committed for some activity resources (such as plant space, number of machines) cannot be changed in the short run.

     D.   **Diseconomies of scale** are increasing average costs with increases in production volume

     E.   **Relevant range** is the range of production levels over which the classification of a cost as fixed or variable is appropriate. Linear equations are good approximations of the behavior of costs within the relevant range.

Readings in Management Accounting

Tom Albright and Harold Roth's "What the Costs of Variability," Reading 4.2 is a good application of cost variability relating to quality.

III.   The Step Function Cost Curve

Step cost functions apply when the linearity assumption of the cost equation does not hold.   See Exhibits 4-10 and 4-11 for illustrations.

A.   **Step function cost curves** are those that increase in relatively narrow discrete steps.

B.   **Step fixed costs** are those that increase in relatively wide discrete steps.

C.   **Step variable costs** are those that increase in relatively narrow discrete steps.

Learning Objective 2:   The ways in which the commitment and consumption of activity resources influence cost variability.   DO MULTIPLE CHOICE QUESTIONS 3 and 4.

IV.   Commitment versus Consumption of Activity Resources

A.   The behavior of costs is contingent on time frame, range of activity levels and other factors.

1.   Another way to think of variable costs is that *they represent resources whose consumption can be adjusted to match the demand placed on them.*

Review Exhibits 14-12 and 4-13.

Learning Objective 3: The normal costs of an activity. DO MULTIPLE CHOICE QUESTION 5.

B.   **Normal cost of an activity** is the average cost at the point where activity demand equals available capacity; cost of providing the resource capacity made available for an activity.

In Equation 4.4, Normal cost can be expressed as:

Normal cost = Regular cost of providing capacity/Capacity made available

This definition of normal cost will surface throughout the text.

Learning Objective 4: The reasons that activity costs tend to be variable in the long run. DO MULTIPLE CHOICE QUESTION 6

Learning Objective 5: The ways to estimate overhead costs for multiple activities supporting the production of multiple products. DO MULTIPLE CHOICE QUESTION 7

Learning Objective 6: The difference between the cost equation and the consumption equation for an activity.

V.   Resource Flexibility and Cost Variability

A.   **Cost behavior** is a description of how costs change with changes in an activity cost driver or production volume.

         1.   A key concept to understand regarding cost behavior is that for some production resources, managers must commit to providing resources often before knowing what the actual demand for them will be. The cost of supplying resources will be incurred regardless of whether they will be fully used.

B.   **Flexible resources** are those which are acquired as needed whose costs vary with production activity

C.	**Discretionary costs** are those that result from strategic and tactical decisions of managers, such that the expenditure levels chosen influence the production volume instead of production volume influencing the consumption of activity resources.

D.	**Committed resources** are those made available for an activity prior to knowing the demand for it. These resources cannot be reduced in case the demand turns out to be less than the capacity made available by the committed resources.

E.	Note that in a well-designed cost system, the changes in the consumption of activity resources must be followed by corresponding changes in the expenditure for the activities.

Readings in Management Accounting

"The Outsourcing Decision," Reading 4.3 presents a timely discussion of the very important, make-or-buy decision. Differential analysis, fixed and variable costs and benchmarking are discussed.

Learning Objective 7. Breakeven analysis. DO MULTIPLE CHOICE QUESTIONS 8, 9 and 10.

VI.	Breakeven Analysis

Breakeven analysis involves determining the level of production at which the profit resulting from one option is at least as large as the profit resulting from an alternative option.

A.	**Contribution margin per unit** is the difference between the revenues and variable costs/price and variable cost per unit.

B.   **Breakeven chart** is a set of graphs depicting the sales revenues and fixed, variable, and total costs.

C.   **Breakeven point** is the point of intersection of the sales revenue curve and the total cost curve.

 Note in Equation 4.9 that the Breakeven point can be expressed as:

Breakeven point (in units) = Fixed costs/Contribution margin per unit

To determine how many units need to be sold to make a target profit, the above equation is modified to be:

Production volume = Fixed costs + target profit/contribution margin per unit.

Learning Objective 8. The way to sketch a planning model that captures the relationship between revenues, costs, and production volumes.

VII.   A Planning Model

Exhibits 4-25, 4-26 and 4-27 outline how a planning model of cost and revenue behavior can be developed. Work through the summary example.

Chapter Quiz/Demonstration Exercises _____

1.   Variable costs:

(a)   do not change with changes in the level of production.
(b)   change with changes in the level of production.
(c)   will never change over any period of time.
(d)   will change every two years.

2.   Rent on a manufacturing facility over a one-year period is an example of a:

(a)   fixed cost.
(b)   variable cost.
(c)   mixed cost.
(d)   step fixed cost.

3.   Resources whose consumption can be adjusted to match the demand placed on them are best represented by _____ costs.

(a)   mixed.
(b)   step variable.
(c)   fixed.
(d)   variable.

4.   The steps in a step fixed cost function are:

(a)   relatively narrow.
(b)   relatively wide.
(c)   extremely wide.
(d)   extremely narrow.

5.   Normal cost is equal to:

(a)   Normal cost of providing capacity/capacity made available.
(b)   Regular cost of providing capacity/normal capacity made available.
(c)   Regular cost of providing capacity/capacity made available.
(d)   Normal cost of providing capacity/normal capacity made available.

6. Activity costs tend to be variable over the long-run because:

    (a)   fixed costs will automatically change over time.
    (b)   mixed and fixed costs will automatically change over time.
    (c)   management has the power to simply change fixed to variable costs whenever its chooses.
    (d)   management has the flexibility to adjust the amount of resources in anticipation of the demand for them.

7. As the _____ _____ becomes larger the demand for different activities may change by different amounts and estimating overhead costs becomes more complex.

    (a)   production volume.
    (b)   resource expenditure.
    (c)   product mix.
    (d)   resource commitment.

8. The breakeven point is:

    (a)   Fixed costs/contribution margin per unit.
    (b)   Fixed and variable costs/contribution margin per unit.
    (c)   Total costs/contribution margin per unit.
    (d)   contribution margin per unit/fixed costs per unit.

9. Thunderbird company has fixed costs of $8,881,760, unit sales price of $150 and unit variable costs of $68. What is the breakeven point (rounded to the nearest whole unit)?

    (a)   59,212 units
    (b)   130,614 units
    (c)   108,314 units
    (d)   Not enough information is given to answer the question.

10. Masefield Company has fixed costs of $6503. Doreen Young, president of the company plans to set the price of Masefield Company's product by adding 33% to its variable cost. Compute the breakeven point.

    (a) $8,671
    (b) $26,012
    (c) $19,706
    (d) $4889

Solutions to Chapter Quiz/Demonstration Exercises_____

1. b.
2. a.
3. d.
4. b.
5. c.
6. d.
7. c.
8. a.
9. c.
10. b.

SYNOPSIS OF *READINGS IN MANAGEMENT ACCOUNTING* AND QUESTIONS TO ASSIGN WITH SUGGESTED ANSWERS

Synopsis of Readings in Management Accounting

The first article for this section is Reading 4.1, Robin Cooper and Robert Kaplan's "*How Cost Accounting Distorts Product Costs.*" In this well-known article, Cooper and Kaplan strongly question the relevance of the traditional cost accounting model and its applicability for product costing. The authors discuss problems with traditional cost accounting including the inadequacy of both variable and full costing methods for accurate product costing, and the failure of both marginal and fixed-cost allocations. Other topics, such as understanding the cost of complexity and transaction costing (an early name for activity-based costing), are introduced. This article helped set the stage for a great deal of research.

The linkages among variations in product and cost standards, cost behavior and quality costs are highlighted in Harold Roth and Tom Albright's article, "*What Are the Costs of Variability,*" Reading 4.2. To illustrate the cost of variability, they cite a number of examples including a study which sought to understand the sources of variation in the quality of paperboard output. In this study, data was collected on variables such as the shifts, crews, grades of product, whether the product was made right after a grade change occurred, etc. The company under study was operating in a capacity-constrained environment and the cost accountants developed a product cost analysis that showed the cost of a products that were lost due to variations in the manufacturing process. Their model included the variable cost of materials and overhead, a fixed cost allocation, and the lost contribution margin. Using this model, the company was able to determine that the cost of certain grades of paperboard exceeded their selling price. The strategic implications of manufacturing products with high variation in product quality became much more evident as a result of the study.

Synopsis of Readings in Management Accounting

Ralph Drtina's article, *"The Outsourcing Decision,"* Reading 4.3, discusses how to determine whether a particular activity should be outsourced. Using a value chain approach, Drtina focuses on outsourcing decisions relating to services. An example that he uses is the decision to outsource fleet maintenance. Three key questions are addressed: (1) Is it possible to purchase the service externally? (2) Does the firm need to control the service activity as would be the case with secret documents or a critical technology? and (3) Is the firm capable of delivering the service at a world-class level of performance? A traditional numerical example that breaks down fixed and variable costs in a make-buy context is provided. Drtina argues that such an analysis ignores qualitative factors and that any outsourcing decision must integrate with the organization's strategy.

Points to Include in Answering Questions from the Readings

1. What does the term "cost of complexity" mean in Cooper and Kaplan's article?

    Student answers should include:
    a. The complexity of costs increases in manufacturing or service organizations as operations require more:
        i.   setups
        ii.   scheduling
        iii. expediting
        iv.   inventory movements
        v.   purchases
        vi.   receipts
    b. This complexity is usually ignored in conventional volume related overhead allocation systems.
    c. Transaction-based or activity-based systems recognize this complexity and provide a better basis for product costing.

2. Describe the "quality loss function" in Roth and Albright's article.

    Student answers should include:
    a. The quality loss function is part of Taguchi's quality philosophy.
    b. The central idea behind this philosophy is that any variability from the target value causes a societal loss.
    c. The quality loss function is a quadratic function in which costs increase as the actual product characteristic deviates from the target value.
    d. The total loss for a period can be calculated by multiplying the average loss per unit by the total number of units.

Points to Include in Answering Questions from the Readings

3.   What are the strategic concerns that Drtina contends must be considered before outsourcing occurs?

Student answers should include:

a.   Technical supremacy - by outsourcing noncritical activities, organizations might learn from the vendor's expertise.

b.   Flexibility - by outsourcing services, some organizations will not be tied to past investments.

c.   Opportunities to coproduce innovation - outsourcing may lead to potential alliances with external vendors.

d.   Too much dependency - organizations have to consider that they might become too dependent on their outsourcing partners. If the partner leaves the organization might lose its competitive advantage.

Recommended Cases

1. Madison Clock Company (A) and (B) in Rotch et al.'s Casebook is a good case to discuss full and variable costing, breakeven analysis and relevant costing.

2. Stalcup Paper Company HBS Case 186-297 is useful for discussing a number of basic costing issues such as product costing and overhead allocation.

3. Industrial Grinders HBS Case 9-175-246 is a little more advanced and deals with relevant costing issues.

Chapter 5

Budgeting for Operations

CENTRAL FOCUS AND LEARNING OBJECTIVES

This chapter focuses on many types and aspects of budgeting including:

1. The role of budgets and budgeting in organizations

2. The elements of the budgeting process and the importance of each

3. The different types of operating budgets and financial budgets, their interrelationships, and their components

4. The way organizations use and interpret budgets

5. What-if and sensitivity analysis - 2 important budgeting tools

6. The types of analyses used by budget planners

7. The role of budgets in service and not-for-profit organizations

Chapter Overview

Chapter 5 presents a broad overview of the budgeting process. The purpose of budgeting for planning and control is discussed as are the many different types of budgets. From the master budget both operating and financial budgets are derived. The details of the many operating budgets are shown and the budgeting process is illustrated.

Focusing on resources, a distinction is made among flexible resources, those that the organization can acquire for the short-term, committed resources those that the organization must acquire for the intermediate term and committed resources necessary for the long term. The chapter also discusses "What-If" and "Sensitivity" analyses within a decision making context. Finally, the role of budgeting in nonprofit and service organizations is presented.

Chapter Outline _____

Budgets are pervasive across all types of organizations. However, some students may not have too much experience in budgeting. One way to garner student interest is to open discussion of this material by asking the class whether anyone has been involved in the budgeting process. Ask volunteers to describe their experiences. Many will probably talk about the budgeting games that went on in their organizations. Refer to this discussion later, especially if you assign C. Bart's article on "Budgeting Gamesmanship" in the Reading Book.

Learning Objective 1: The role of budgets and budgeting in organizations
DO MULTIPLE CHOICE PROBLEM 1.

I.   The Role of Budgets and Budgeting

    A.   A **budget** is a quantitative model or a summary of the expected consequences of the organization's short-term operating activities.

    B.   A **model** is a representation. In this case, budgets are a model of the organization.

    C.   **Budgeting** is the process of preparing budgets and requires the use of forecasts, knowing how activities cause costs and the ability to integrate the organization's activities.

    D.   Budgeting supports the management functions of planning and coordinating activities and communicates the organization's short-term goals to its members.

 Review the key role of budgeting as shown in Exhibit 5-1

II.   Types of Budgets

Learning Objective 2: The elements of the budgeting process and the importance of each. DO MULTIPLE CHOICE PROBLEM 2.

Learning Objective 3: The different types of operating budgets and financial budgets, their interrelationships, and their components. DO MULTIPLE CHOICE PROBLEMS 3 AND 4.

 The following budgets all flow from the master budget.

A.   An **operating budget** is one that summarizes the financial results expected from the chosen operating plans.

  1.   A **sales plan** is a document that summarizes planned sales for each product.

  2.   A **capital spending plan** is an operating plan that specifies when long-term capital expenditures such as acquisitions for buildings and special-purpose equipment must be made to meet activity objectives.

  3.   A **production plan** is an operating plan that identifies all required production.

  4.   A **materials purchasing plan** is an operating plan that schedules purchasing activities.

  5.   A **labor hiring and training plan** is an operating plan that schedules the hiring, releasing, and training of people that the organization must have to achieve its activity objectives.

  6.   An **administrative and discretionary spending plan** is an operating plan that summarizes administrative and discretionary expenditures.

B.   A **financial budget** is one that summarizes activities such as production quantities and labor requirements.

C.   A **pro forma statement** is a forecasted or estimated statement.

 Students should understand the differences among these types of budgets. Refer to Exhibit 5-2 for the linkages among the many types of budgets. We will refer to this exhibit many times during the chapter.

Readings in Management Accounting

Takeo Tanaka's article, "Target Costing at Toyota (Reading 5.1) illustrates how cost planning occurs at the large Japanese auto manufacturer. The article has some technical elements but is a very useful counterpoint to the traditional budgeting model presented in Chapter 5.

II.   The Budgeting Process

Learning Objective 4: The way organizations use and interpret budgets. DO MULTIPLE CHOICE PROBLEMS 5 AND 6.

 Review the budgeting process example, Gael's Tole Art, Buoy Division to understand how the process works. Work through all of the Exhibits beginning with Exhibits 5-5 and 5-6.

A. A **demand forecast** is an estimate of the market demand, or sales potential, for a product under specified conditions. The budgeting process begins with a demand forecast.

B. The sales plan is then matched with inventory policy and capacity levels and a **production plan** is determined.

　　1. **A chase demand strategy** is a policy of producing for demand. When production occurs exactly, and only, when the units are required, this strategy is called a just-in-time production strategy.

C. **Aggregate planning** is an approximate determination of whether the organization has the capacity to undertake a proposed production plan (also called rough-cut planning).

D. **Spending plans** are developed to purchase raw materials, hire and train new employees. There are many such plans.

　　1. A **discretionary expenditure** is an expenditure whose short-term cost is not dictated directly by the proposed level of activities (e.g., advertising and research and development).

　　2. An **engineered expenditure** is one whose short-term cost is directly determined by the proposed level of activity. Engineered expenditures reflect product design and process design (e.g. materials costs and the cost of causal labor).

 The distinctions among flexible resources and both types of committed resources below should be stressed.

E. There are three major types of resources and that organizations acquire that will determine their level of monthly production capacity.

　　1. **Flexible resources** are those that the organization can acquire in the short-term. Examples include many types of materials.

2. **Committed resources** that the organization must acquire for the intermediate term include labor.

3. **Committed resources** that the organization must acquire for the long term. These include plant and equipment.

F. Understanding the production plan involves the idea that production is the minimum of demand and capacity. In equation form this is:

Production = Minimum (total demand, production capacity)

G. Financial plans including the projected balance sheet, income statement and cash flow statement are extremely important.

1. A **Line of credit** is a short-term financing arrangement, with a prespecified limit, between an organization and a financial institution.

 Continue with the Gael's Tole Art, Buoy Division example, and review Exhibits 5-8 to 5-16 on the above key financial statements.

Readings in Management Accounting

Reading 5.2, Christopher Bart's "Budgeting Gamesmanship," presents a number of behavioral implications of budgeting that are not covered in the chapter (however, some aspects are discussed in Chapter 14). If you began the class by having students discuss their experiences, this article may be especially useful and pertinent.

Learning Objective 5: What-if and sensitivity analysis - 2 important budgeting tools. DO MULTIPLE CHOICE QUESTION 7.

III.   What-if Analysis

A.   **What-if analysis** is a strategy that uses a model to predict the results of varying a model's key parameters. Through this method a number of questions can be raised concerning specific changes to variables and their effects on the key financial indicators.

Learning Objective 6: The types of analyses used by budget planners. DO MULTIPLE CHOICE QUESTIONS 8 AND 9.

B.   **Sensitivity analysis** is an analytical tool that involves selectively varying key estimates of a plan or budget. Sensitivity analysis allows planners to identify the estimates that have critical effects on decisions based on that plan. If small changes in plan parameters (estimates and relationships) produce large changes in decisions or results, the plan is said to be sensitive to the estimates.

Readings in Management Accounting

"Why Budgets Are Bad for Business," Thomas Stewart's article from *Fortune* (Reading 5.3) illustrates the pros and cons of budgeting. It is a good article to summarize both the procedural aspects of budgeting and the ways that people use and interpret them.

IV.   The Role of Budgeting in Service and Nonprofit Organizations

Learning Objective 7: The role of budgets in service and not-for-profit organizations. DO MULTIPLE CHOICE QUESTION 10.

A.   An **appropriation** is an authorized spending limit.

B.   A **periodic budget** is one that is prepared for a specified period of time, usually one year. As each budget period ends, the organization prepares a new budget for the next one.

C.   **Continuous budgeting** is a process that plans for a specified period of time, usually 1 year, and organizes a budget into budget subintervals, usually a month or a quarter. As each budget subinterval ends, the organization drops the completed subinterval from the budget and adds the next budget subinterval.

D.   **Zero-base budgeting** is an approach to developing appropriations for discretionary expenditures that assumes that the starting point for each discretionary expenditure item is zero.

E.   **Incremental budgeting** is an approach to developing appropriations for discretionary expenditures that assumes that the starting point for each discretionary expenditure item is the amount spent on it in the previous budget.

F.   **Project funding** is an approach to developing appropriations for discretionary expenditures that organizes appropriations into a package that focuses on achieving some defined output. For example, an organization might fund a project designed to identify and evaluate its practiced organization ethics.

Chapter Quiz/Demonstration Exercises _____

1. Each of the following are part of the yearly planning, control and budgeting process, EXCEPT:

    (a) Develop long-term strategy.
    (b) Develop long-term operating activities.
    (c) Measure and assess performance.
    (d) Reevaluate objectives, goals, strategy and plans.

2. The projected balance sheet and the projected income statement also are called:

    (a) capital spending financial statements.
    (b) the master budget.
    (c) operating budgets.
    (d) pro forma financial statements.

3. Operating budgets or plans include the following, EXCEPT:

    (a) capital spending plan.
    (b) production plan.
    (c) financial investment plan.
    (d) materials purchasing plan.

4. The administrative and discretionary spending plan includes each of the following, EXCEPT:

    (a) investment in building and equipment plans.
    (b) staffing plans.
    (c) research and development plans.
    (d) advertising plans.

5. The budgeting process is driven by _____.

    (a) the production plan.
    (b) aggregate planning.
    (c) the demand forecast.
    (d) the spending plan.

6.   Which of the following is not a type of resource used to determine monthly production capacity?

(a)   Flexible resources acquired for the short-term.
(b)   Flexible resources acquired for the long-term.
(c)   Committed resources acquired for the intermediate term.
(d)   Committed resources acquired for the long term.

7.   Production is:

(a)   the maximum of total demand and production capacity.
(b)   the maximum of total supply of raw materials and production capacity.
(c)   the minimum of total supply of raw materials and production capacity.
(d)   the minimum of total demand and production capacity

8.   Each of the following is an important characteristic of a model that underlies what-if analysis, EXCEPT:

(a)   The model must be complete.
(b)   The model must reflect relationships accurately.
(c)   The model must have tested for at least 7 years.
(d)   The model must use reasonable estimates.

9.   If forecasting errors have a critical effect on the production plan, planners say that the model is _____ to that estimate.

(a)   unrelated.
(b)   insensitive.
(c)   related.
(d)   sensitive.

10.   Zero-based budgeting ideas do not apply to _____ costs, which are short-term costs that have an identifiable relationship with some activity level.

(a)   engineered.
(b)   discretionary.
(c)   incremental.
(d)   continuous.

Solutions to Chapter Quiz/Demonstration Exercises_____

1.   b.
2.   d.
3.   c.
4.   a.
5.   c.
6.   b.
7.   d.
8.   c.
9.   d.
10.   a.

SYNOPSIS OF *READINGS IN MANAGEMENT ACCOUNTING* AND QUESTIONS TO ASSIGN WITH SUGGESTED ANSWERS

Synopsis of Readings in Management Accounting

Takeo Tanaka's "*Target Costing at Toyota*," presents an interesting discussion of the cost planning process at the well-known automobile manufacturer (Reading 5.1). Tanaka contends that many Japanese managers now believe that the biggest opportunities for cost reduction can be located at the product planning and development stages rather than at the production stage. The concept of target costing is used to reduce costs at these early stages.

Using information from interviews with Toyota's chief engineer and controller, Tanaka describes the two broad categories of product development. The first is the development of new types of automobiles, while the second focuses on making complete or minor changes to existing cars. For budgeting purposes, the idea of setting cost reduction goals and then achieving those goals through design changes is central to the target costing notion.

Reading 5.2, Christopher Bart's "*Budgeting Gamesmanship*," describes the games that managers play with their budgets. Bart defines budgeting gamesmanship as "the deliberate and premeditated manipulation of current year sales, cost and profit forecasts by product managers to project an overly conservative image into their product budgets." Using interview and company data from eight large diversified companies, Bart documents how and why managers pad their budgets. Two key factors for why such padding occurs are the fear that senior management will arbitrarily slash their submitted budgets and their own concerns about uncertainty in the competitive environment in which they work.

Synopsis of Readings in Management Accounting

In "*Why Budgets Are Bad for Business*," Thomas Stewart (Reading 5.3) continues with the theme developed by Bart and adds a few more cautionary notes when trying to understand the budgeting process. Stewart argues that while necessary, budgets focus attention and control on the line items shown on the budget and often ignore the key underlying concepts such as quality and customer service and satisfaction that make a business successful. Consistent with Bart's article, managers can become extremely preoccupied with playing budgeting games. If managers are intent on "making budget" as their key goal and organizational rewards are contingent on this goal, then they may never be able to be forward looking and innovative.

Points to Include in Answering Questions from the Readings

1.   What does Tanaka say is the key difference between target costing and Kaizen costing?

Student answers should include:
a.   At Toyota, the cost goals for design are met through target costing.
b.   The cost goals for mass production are met using cost kaizen.
c.   The two concepts work together at different stages of the life cycle of an automobile.

Points to Include in Answering Questions from the Readings

2. What are some of the factors that constrain the budget games discussed by Christopher Bart?

   Student answers should include:
   a. Senior management can look at historical spending trends of each product and if current expenses are out of line they would investigate.
   b. Senior management could also tell product managers what their target profit had to be. Often this would eliminate any cushions.
   c. In some cases a senior manager would ask other managers where the hedges were and eliminate them. It seems that the more profit pressure the more senior management would seek out the cushions.

3. In Stewart's article, what does Ronald Mitsch, a 3M vice president mean when he says, "Plan first, budget later"?

   Student answers should include:
   a. Mitsch means that there are some traditional budget items that should be handled over the long-term, and not relegated to short-term pressure.
   b. For instance, cost reduction should be viewed over a five-year horizon because one way to reduce costs is to make sound investments in new methods or equipment. Using a one-year budget horizon to deal with cost reduction could result in significant strategic errors.

Recommended Cases

1. Blackheath Manufacturing Company and Blackheath Manufacturing Company-Revisited in Rotch et al.'s Casebook are straightforward, but comprehensive cases on the mechanics of budgeting.

2. Hanson Industries (A) and (B), HBS Cases 9-179-076 and 9-179-077 and accompanying teaching notes (5-180-164) and (5-180-164) are a good introduction to budgeting in a small, but fast-growing company.

Chapter 6

Basic Product Costing Systems

CENTRAL FOCUS AND LEARNING OBJECTIVES

In this chapter fundamental concepts relating to basic product costing systems are presented. These include:

1.. The use of job bid sheets to estimate product costs in a job order costing system

2. The use of overhead rates to apply overhead to products

3. The reasons that cost systems with multiple labor and overhead rates give different estimates of product costs than cost systems with a single rate

4. The evaluation of a cost system to understand whether it is likely to distort product costs

5. The relevance of recording actual costs and comparing them with estimated costs

6. The analysis of variances between actual and estimated costs, and including first-and second-level variances

7. The importance of conversion costs and the measurement of costs in multistage, continuous-processing industries

8. The differences between job order costing and multi-stage processing systems

Chapter Overview _____

Chapter 6 introduces basic product costing systems. Beginning with job order costing systems, constructing job bid sheets, determining markup rate and dealing with problems with fluctuating overhead rates are discussed.

Recording actual job costs is considered next and examples of materials requisition notes, worker time cards and job cost sheets are presented. Determining first and second-level variances of the differences between estimated and actual costs follows.

In the final section of the chapter, multistage product costing for continuous processing industries is discussed and the concept of conversion costs introduced.

Chapter Outline _____

This chapter considers the familiar topics of job order and process costing, however, you will find differences from a more traditional treatment. As an example, note that overhead rate is defined as normal cost of support activity divided by normal level of cost driver.

Learning Objective 1. The use of job bid sheets to estimate product costs in a job order costing system. DO MULTIPLE CHOICE QUESTION 1.

I. Job Order Costing Systems

A. **Job order costing system** is a system for estimating costs of products in organizations that produce several different types of products. More specifically, a job order costing system estimates costs of producing products for different jobs required for customer orders.

B. A **job bid sheet** is a format for estimating job costs.

Review Exhibit 6-1 for an example of a job bid sheet. Note panels 2 and 3 for standard engineering and industrial engineering specifications.

C. **Job costs** are the total of direct material, direct labor and overhead costs estimated for, or identified with, a job.

D. **Markup or margin** is the amount of profit added to estimated job costs to arrive at bid price.

E. The markup rate may be contingent on the **rate of return** that the organization has specified. The rate of return is the ratio of net income to investment also called return on investment.

Learning Objective 2: The use of overhead rates to apply overhead to products. DO MULTIPLE CHOICE QUESTION 2.

F.   Determining overhead rates and costs have become very important. **Overhead cost pools** are those identified categories of overhead costs; each category has a separate rate, that is used.

G.   The **Overhead rate** is the rate at which overhead costs are applied to individual jobs. It is the ratio of the normal cost for a support activity accumulated in a cost pool to the normal level of the cost driver for the activity. See equation 6.1.

H.   A general principle related to the **number of cost pools** is that separate cost pools should be used if the cost or productivity of resources is different and if the pattern of demand varies across resources.

Learning Objective 3: The reasons that cost systems with multiple labor and overhead rates give different estimates of product costs than cost systems with a single rate. DO MULTIPLE CHOICE QUESTIONS 3 and 4.

I.   Determining an overhead rate as the budgeted (or actual) cost per unit of the budgeted (or actual) use of that activity results in misleading product costs. The correct method for determining the overhead rate is to estimate the normal cost per unit of the activity level committed.

     See Exhibit 6.2 for an illustration.

Learning Objective 4: The evaluation of a cost system to understand whether it is likely to distort product costs. DO MULTIPLE CHOICE QUESTIONS 5 AND 6.

A comprehensive illustration for Learning Objective 4 is provided by Archie's Auto example. Review this example paying particular attention to Exhibits 6-3 through 6-7.

Learning Objective 5: The relevance of recording actual costs and comparing them with estimated costs. DO MULTIPLE CHOICE QUESTION 7.

II.   Recording Actual Job Costs

This section discusses the actual procedures for recording job costs.

A.   A **materials requisition note** is a note telling the stores department to issue materials to the shop floor in order to commence production

B.   **Worker time cards** record the hours spent by each worker each day or week on different jobs

C.   A **job cost sheet** is a format for recording actual job costs.

 Review Exhibits 6-8, 9 and 10 which provide examples of each of the documents discussed above.

Readings in Management Accounting

Reading 6.1, Robin Cooper's well-known article "Does Your Company Need a New Cost System," fleshes out many of the problems with basic costing systems and discusses when a traditional cost system should be replaced.

III.   Basic Variance Analysis

Variances are differences between actual and estimated costs and are a necessary step for managers who are attempting to understand why a difference occurred.

A.   **First-level variance** is the difference between actual and estimated costs for a cost item such as direct labor or direct materials.

1.   A **favorable variance**, signified by an "F," means that actual costs were less than estimated costs.

2.   An **unfavorable variance**, signified by a "U," means that actual costs were greater than estimated costs.

B.   **Second-level variance** is further analysis of a first-level variance.

For instance, direct materials can be broken down into efficiency (use) and price variances. The formulae for calculating second-level variances are as follows:

1.   The **direct materials price variance is:**

(AP - SP) * AQ

where

AP = actual price of materials
SP = estimated or standard price of materials
AQ = actual quantity of materials used

2.   The **direct materials usage variance** is:

(AQ - SQ) * SP

where

AQ = actual quantity of materials used

SQ = estimated or standard quantity of materials required

SP = estimated or standard price of materials

3.   By summing both the price and usage variances we get the **total variance** or actual cost minus estimated cost.

Usage variance + Price variance =

$$= (AQ - SQ) * SP + (AP - SP) * AQ$$

$$= (AP * AQ) - (SQ * SP)$$

4.   Note that there are times when *the amount of materials purchased is different from that used.* This is because materials often are purchased in large quantities and stored until needed. Thus, it is common to separate out the material price variance at the time of purchase and charge jobs for materials only at their standard prices. See Equation 6.5.

Direct labor cost also can be broken down into wage rate and efficiency variances

5.   The **wage rate variance is:**

$$(AR - SR) * AH$$

where

AR = actual wage rate

SR = estimated or standard number of direct labor hours

AH = actual number of direct labor hours

6.   The **efficiency variance** is:

$$(AH - SH) * SR$$

where

AH = actual number of direct labor hours

SH = estimated or standard number of direct labor hours

SR = estimated or standard number of direct labor hours

3. By summing both the wage rate and efficiency variances we get the **total variance** or actual cost minus estimated cost.

Usage variance + Price variance =

$$= (AH - SH) * SR + (AR - SR) * AH$$

$$= (AR * AH) - (SR * SH)$$

 Review Exhibits 6-11 through 6-13 on the basic mechanics of variance analyses

Readings in Management Accounting

Norm Raffish's article, "How Much Does That Product Really Co$t," Reading 6.2, can be used here. It provides a good transition from basic product costing to newer methods such as activity-based costing.

Learning Objective 7: The importance of conversion costs and the measurement of costs in multistage, continuous-process industries. DO MULTIPLE CHOICE QUESTION 10.

Learning Objective 8: The differences between job order costing and multi-stage processing systems.

V.   Multistage Process Costing Systems

A.   A **multistage process costing system** is a system for determining product costs in multistage processing industries such as chemicals, basic metals, pharmaceuticals, etc.

1.   With this method the first step is to **assess costs for each stage of the process** and then to assign costs to individual products.

2.   A common feature of process costing is that the products that are produced are relatively **homogeneous**.

3.   Since costs are measured only at process stages, **cost variances** are determined only at the level of the process stages and not at the individual job level.

4.   **Conversion costs** are costs of production labor and support activities to convert the materials or product at each process stage.

Exhibits 6-15 through 6-18 illustrate process costing. At the end of the chapter, ask students to describe the differences between job order and process costing.

Readings in Management Accounting

William Turk's "Management Accounting Revitalized: The Harley-Davidson Experience," Reading 6.3, provides a good wrap-up to this chapter by contrasting Harley-Davidson's transition from a basic product costing system to one that is much more compatible with their JIT system.

Chapter Quiz/Demonstration Exercises _____

1. Each of the following statements is true about job order costing systems, EXCEPT:

   (a) A job order costing system is a method used for estimating product costs in firms that have several distinct products.

   (b) A job order costing system estimates costs of manufacturing products for different jobs required for customer orders.

   (c) A job order costing system relies on the concept of conversion costs.

   (d) A job order costing system provides the means to estimate costs so that bids can be prepared.

2. From the following information determine a 20% markup on job H1. For H1, direct materials are $4,000, direct labor is $5,500 and overhead costs are $7,400.

   (a) $11,400
   (b) $20,280
   (c) $15,480
   (d) $13680

3. From the following information calculate the overhead rate for cost pool ABKY from the following information: The rate of return is 15%; normal cost of support activity is $7,700, the markup percentage is 18% and the normal level of the cost driver is 200.

   (a) $165.00
   (b) $36.00
   (c) $30.00
   (d) $38.50

4. The correct method of determining overhead rates is:

   (a) to estimate the normal cost per unit of the activity level committed.

   (b) to estimate the normal cost per unit of the activity level available.

   (c) to estimate the actual cost per unit of the activity level available.

   (d) to estimate the actual cost per unit of the activity level committed.

5.   Choose the best answer given the following scenario. One may to tell whether your overhead allocation system is distorting product costs is after performing an activity analysis you discover that:

(a)   the most complex products you produce are overpriced and the simplest to produce are underpriced.
(b)   the most complex products you produce are underpriced and the simplest to produce are overpriced.
(c)   the most complex products you produce are overpriced as are the simplest to produce.
(d)   the most complex products you produce are underpriced as are the simplest to produce.

6.   Worker time cards:

(a)   instruct shop floor personnel when to request materials from its suppliers.
(b)   inform management when each worker will go on vacation.
(c)   instruct workers when to bring materials to the shop floor to commence production.
(d)   record the amount of time workers spend on each job.

7.   Each of the following is essential to recording actual job costs, EXCEPT:

(a)   Cost estimate for customer job.
(b)   Materials requisition note.
(c)   Worker time cards.
(d)   Job cost sheet.

8.   Which of the formulae below correctly illustrates the calculation for the efficiency variance for direct labor?

(a) $(AR - SR) * AH$.
(b) $(AH - SH) * SR$.
(c) $(AR - SR) * SH$.
(d) $(AH - SH) * AR$.

9.   Given the following information calculate the materials usage variance for direct materials: AP = $300, SP = $315; AQ = 12.

   (a)   15U
   (b)   180U
   (c)   180F
   (d)   15F

10.   Total costs of all activities performed at each stage of a process costing system are referred to as:

   (a)   direct costs.
   (b)   first-level costs.
   (c)   overhead costs.
   (d)   conversion costs.

Solutions to Chapter Quiz/Demonstration Exercises_____

1. c.
2. b.
3. d.
4. a.
5. c.
6. d.
7. a.
8. b.
9. c.
10. d.

SYNOPSIS OF *READINGS IN MANAGEMENT ACCOUNTING* AND QUESTIONS TO ASSIGN WITH SUGGESTED ANSWERS

Synopsis of Readings in Management Accounting

Reading 6.1, Robin Cooper's "*Does Your Company Need a New Cost System*," poses a critical question for managers: "Do I really know what my products cost?" Answering this question will allow managers to determine whether their costing system is reporting accurate product costs. In order to address this question, Cooper suggests that managers look for symptoms that often point to poor system design. For example, one symptom of a poor system occurs when an firm's customers completely ignore price increases, even though the firm's manufacturing costs haven't changed. In this instance, the cost system may be underestimating product costs and thus the associated markup is still below market. Cooper outlines a number of other design flaws that managers should understand as they attempt to develop more accurate systems.

Consistent with Robin Cooper's article, in "*How Much Does That Product Really Co$t*," (Reading 6.2), Norm Raffish argues that the business world has changed so much that traditional cost accounting is no longer applicable. For one thing the relative proportions of what goes into product costs have changed significantly with direct labor content dropping to between 5 and 15%, materials content falling between 45% and 55% and overhead soaring to between 30% and 50%. Raffish builds the case for activity-based costing as a much more accurate method for determining (among other things) more accurate product costs. The article is based in part on the research of Computer-Aided Manufacturing-International (now the Consortium for Advanced Manufacturing-International, CAM-I).

Synopsis of Readings in Management Accounting

William Turk presents an extremely interesting account of Harley-Davidson's transformation of both its traditional manufacturing and cost accounting systems. In Reading 6.3, "*Management Accounting Revitalized: The Harley-Davidson Experience,*" Turk shows that, after management had installed a just-in-time manufacturing system, the accountants realized that their traditional product costing system was becoming more and more obsolete. One of the key problems was with the direct labor based method of assigning overhead. As the JIT method reduces the amount of inventory this, in turn, reduces the amount of direct labor dollars. A consequence is that the amount of overhead absorbed also decreases which gives the appearance that performance is deteriorating. Turk describes the process of education that Harley Davidson's accountants went through to break their fixation on using direct labor dollars as the basis of allocation and the new management accounting system that developed.

Points to Include in Answering Questions from the Readings

1.   What are three of the design flaws that Cooper says may exist in a costing system?

Student answers should include:
- a.   Only direct labor hours, or dollars, are used to allocated overhead from cost centers (pools) to products.
- b.   Profit margins cannot be explained easily.
- c.   Some products that you sell but are not sold by competitors have high reported margins.
- d.   The results of bids are hard to explain.
- e.   The competitor's high-volume products are priced at apparently unrealistically low levels.
- f.   Vendor bids for parts are considerably lower than expected.
- g.   Cost pools are too large and contain machines that have very different overhead cost structures.

Points to Include in Answering Questions from the Readings

1.   (continued)

     h.   The cost of marketing and delivering the product varies dramatically by distribution channel, and yet the cost accounting system effectively ignores marketing costs.

2.   In Norm Raffish's paper, what are the five steps involved in product life-cycle costs? How much of a product's cost is committed after the design phase and why is this number important?

    Student answers should include:

    a.   The five steps are:
          i.   product planning, concept design
          ii.   preliminary design
          iii.   detailed design and prototype
          iv.   production
          v.   distribution and logistics support

    b.   Approximately 85% of the cost of a new product is committed after the design phase. Thus manufacturing can only influence about 15% of the cost and the traditional costing system does not really account for the other 85%.

3.   William Turk states that "direct labor reporting in a JIT environment adds cost without adding value." What are the reasons for this statement?

    Student answers should include:

    a.   Direct labor reporting consumes a great deal of operator time filling out labor tickets.
    b.   Direct labor reporting also consumers supervisors' time as they have to review the tickets.
    c.   Timekeepers have to be paid to enter labor data and review the data outputs for accuracy.
    d.   Cost accountants have to review the direct labor and variance data and record it for inventory valuation and expense accounting.
    e.   Financial analysts have to review, audit and edit the inventory valuation and expense charges.

Recommended Cases

1. Narnia, Inc. is a basic case in product costing and problems with misallocation of overhead. The case is contained in Rotch et al.'s casebook.

2. The Bridgeton Industries case can also be used in this chapter for a medium difficulty case on determining overhead rates and product costs (HBS case 190-085 and the accompanying teaching note 5-191-168).

3. Sentry Group is a good case to illustrate how a company moved from a poorly designed cost system to an activity-based system (HBS Case 9-191-027 and teaching note 5-191-195).

Chapter 7

Two-Stage Allocations and Activity-Based Costing Systems

CENTRAL FOCUS AND LEARNING OBJECTIVES

In this chapter the rationale for both two-stage allocations and activity-based costing is presented. Topics include:

1. The difference between production and service departments

2. The process of allocating service department costs to production departments

3. The two stages of cost allocations and the difference between them

4. The reason why conventional two-stage allocation methods often distort production costs

5. The use of activity-based costing system to estimate product costs

6. The reason why activity-based costing systems avoid distortions in allocating batch-related costs

7. The method for assigning selling and distribution costs to products

---

Chapter Overview

This chapter begins by developing the rationale for two-stage cost allocations. First, the differences between production and service departments are discussed. Conventional product costing systems assign indirect costs to jobs or products in two stages. In the first stage, indirect costs are associated with various production and service departments. Then, all service department costs are allocated to production departments. In the second stage, the total indirect costs for the production departments are assigned to individual jobs or products based on predetermined overhead rates.

Details about stage one allocation methods such as the direct, sequential and reciprocal allocation methods are presented, followed by stage two allocations and the potential distortions in costs that can arise with them. Activity-based costing (ABC) is presented next as a way to overcome many of the problems of traditional two-stage allocations. A key advantage of ABC is that cost drivers are developed that directly link the activities performed to the products manufactured. Implications for selling and distribution activities also are discussed.

Chapter Outline _____

 The treatment of two-stage allocations and activity-based costing in this chapter is quite detailed and well-structured. You may want to spend significant time on each of the two stages of two-stage allocations. This will help to motivate the power of ABC.

I.   The Two Stage Cost Allocation Method

 This section discusses conventional methods of allocation and begins with a discussion of how departmental structure affects allocation methods.

Learning Objective 1: The difference between production departments and service departments. DO MULTIPLE CHOICE QUESTION 1.

A.   Effects of Departmental Structure on Allocation

1.   **Production departments** are those directly responsible for some of the work of converting raw materials into finished products. Examples include casting, stamping, machining, assembly and packing departments.

2.   **Service departments** are those performing activities that support production, but are not responsible for any of the conversion stages. Examples include machine maintenance, machine setup and production scheduling.

Learning Objective 2: The process of allocating service department costs to production departments. DO MULTIPLE CHOICE QUESTION 2.

Exhibit 7-1 illustrates the process of allocating service department costs to production departments. Students should understand this exhibit as it will help them later to grasp ABC.

Learning Objective 3: The two stages of cost allocations and the differences between them. DO MULTIPLE CHOICE QUESTIONS 3 and 4.

B. The Two Stage Method

1. Conventional product costing systems assign indirect costs to products or jobs in 2 stages.

2. In **Stage 1,** indirect costs are identified with production and service departments. Then all service department costs are allocated to the production departments.

a. **The direct allocation method** is a simple method to allocate service department costs to production departments that ignores interdependencies between service departments.

Follow the Medequip example to understand stage 1 cost allocations. Exhibits 7-2 through 7-6 illustrate the process.

b. **The sequential allocation method** is a method that recognizes interdependencies between service departments and allocates service department costs 1 service department at a time in a sequential order. See Appendix 7-1 for more details on this method.

c. **The reciprocal allocation method** is a method to determine service department cost allocations simultaneously, recognizing the reciprocity between pairs of service departments. See Appendix 7-1 for more details on this method.

3.   In **Stage 2** the system assigns all of the accumulated indirect costs for the production department to individual products or jobs based on predetermined overhead rates. The allocation bases for production departments often are unit-based measures and include the number of units produced, the number of direct labor hours or cost and the number of machine hours.

 Stage 2 allocations are well illustrated in the Medequip example in Exhibits 7-7 through 7-15.

Learning Objective 4. The reason that conventional two-stage allocation methods often distort production costs. DO MULTIPLE CHOICE QUESTIONS 5 and 6.

II.   Distortions Caused By Two-Stage Allocations

There are two major reasons why two-stage allocations can distort product costs.

A.   Allocations are based on unit-related measures.

B.   Consumption ratios of resources for products often are different from those based on unit-related measures.

For example a distortion can arise if a unit-related measure such as machine hours is used for overhead allocation even though some products are produced in larger batches requiring fewer setup costs, and thus consume differential amounts of overhead costs. Note in Exhibit 7-11 that the two products have the same number of machine hours, but A is produced in larger batch sizes. Under the two-stage method, both A and B will receive the same overhead costs even though B requires more setups.

Readings in Management Accounting

Terence Pare's, "A New Tool for Managing Costs," is a very good introductory article on activity-based costing (Reading 7.1).

III.   Activity-Based Costing Systems

A.   Distortions like those described for two-stage systems can be overcome by designing a costing system that uses the actual cost driver for each activity to assign costs directly to products. This kind of a system is called an activity-based costing system.

 Activity-based costing is an extremely important method which has changed the way that many decision-makers think about management accounting. Work through Exhibits 7-12 through 7-15.

B.   **Activity-based costing systems** are costing systems based on cost drivers that link activities performed to products and allocate overhead activity costs directly to products using these cost drivers.

 Ask students if they know the differences between two-stage allocation methods and activity-based costing? How does ABC overcome the distortions caused by the two-stage method?

Readings in Management Accounting

Students often lament that there are not enough applications of ABC to service organizations. In chapter 7 of the Readings Book, three examples of ABC in service organizations are provided. Reading 7.2, "Activity-Based Costing in Service Industries by William Rotch is a good overview article. David Carlson and Mark Young's piece, "Activity-Based Total Quality Management at American Express," (Reading 7.3) illustrates an integrated ABC and TQM system. Lawrence Carr's "Unbundling the Cost of Hospitalization," discusses the application of ABC in a private rehabilitation hospital (Reading 7.4).

IV.   Selling and Distribution Activities

Selling and distribution costs are being linked more and more to product costs.

A.   Many conventional systems either completely exclude selling and distribution and other nonmanufacturing costs from product costs or use arbitrary methods such as relative sales value to assign them.

B.   Today because of the new emphasis on customer orientation and technological innovation for competitive advantage, selling and distribution costs are being examined more closely. The general idea is to determine whether some products consume greater selling and distribution costs than others, and to determine whether some of these costs should be included in product costs.

Exhibits 7-16 through 7-18 illustrate how selling and distribution costs can be analyzed from an activity-based costing viewpoint.

V. Appendix 7-1

    A. The Sequential Allocation

        1. The **sequential method of allocation** is used if no 2 service departments consume a significant proportion of the services produced by the other department.

        2. Under this method, the service departments are arranged in order so that a service department can receive costs allocated from another service department only before its own costs are allocated to other departments.

        3. The costs of the service department that provides the highest percentage of its service to other service departments are allocated first. This procedure continues with the department providing the lowest percentage of its service going last. Once a service department's costs are allocated, no costs of any other department can be allocated back to it.

        4. The total cost of service departments allocated to other departments are the directly identified costs with that department plus the amount(s) allocated earlier from other service departments.

 See Exhibits 7A-1 and 7A-2 for an illustration of the sequential allocation method.

    B. The Reciprocal Allocation Method

        1. When there are interactions between different service departments (e.g. when both provide service to each other) the **reciprocal method** is used.

2.	The sequential method cannot work in this situation because allocating the service costs of department A to B, both of which provide service to each other, means that B will then have to allocate a portion of A's cost back to it. This cannot work because all of A's costs have already been allocated. Thus A would still have unallocated costs in it.

3.	Solving this problem requires using simultaneous equations as shown in the text.

 Work through equations 7A.1 and 7A.2 in the text on reciprocal allocation and Exhibits 7A-3 and 7A-4 for an illustration of the reciprocal allocation method.

Chapter Quiz/Demonstration Exercises _____

1. All service department costs are _____ costs because they do not arise from direct production activities.

    (a) direct.
    (c) indirect.
    (c) variable.
    (d) fixed.

2. In stage two of the conventional cost allocation procedure:

    (a) the system identifies indirect costs with various production and service departments.
    (b) all service department costs are allocated to production departments.
    (c) accumulated indirect costs for production departments are assigned to individual jobs or products.
    (d) accumulated production department costs are assigned to service departments and then assigned to individual jobs or products.

3. Which of the following methods recognizes the interdependencies between service departments and allocates service department costs one service department at a time.

    (a) Direct allocation.
    (b) Reciprocal allocation.
    (c) Stage 2 allocation.
    (d) Sequential allocation.

4. Below are four activities and four allocation bases. Which of the four has the weakest link between activity and allocation basis?

	Activity	Allocation Basis
(a)	Machine setup	Number of setups
(b)	Machine maintenance	Book value of machines
(c)	Lighting on shop floor	Number of kilowatt hours
(d)	Quality control	Square feet of floor space

5. One major reason that two-stage allocations lead to cost distortion is that many allocations are based on _____-_____ measures.

   (a) unit-related.
   (b) batch-related.
   (c) product-related.
   (d) facility-related.

6. Which of the following is a batch-related cost driver?

   (a) Number of machine hours.
   (b) Number of setups
   (c) Number of engineering changes.
   (d) Number of direct labor hours.

7. deCastro Company produces two products SP24 and SP25. Each is assigned $25.00 in setup costs by a conventional accounting system. After an activity analysis it is revealed that SP25 requires 45 fewer minutes in setup time than SP 24. Under an ABC system SP25 is:

   (a) undercosted.
   (b) overcosted.
   (c) fairly costed.
   (d) accurately costed.

8. Activity-based costing develops cost drivers that:

   (a) directly link the activities performed to the products produced.
   (b) indirectly link the activities performed to the products produced.
   (a) do not take setup activities into account.
   (b) quality inspection activities into account.

9. Selling and distribution costs include each of the following, EXCEPT:

   (a) marketing management.
   (b) distributing sales catalogs.
   (c) industrial engineering changes.
   (d) shipping.

10. Selling and distribution costs may be considered as part of product costing because:

(a) generally accepted accounting principles now require it.

(b) customers think its the best way to handle such costs.

(c) traditional management accounting principles demand it.

(d) the demand for the selling and distribution activities placed by different products for different customers needs to be reflected.

Solutions to Chapter Quiz/Demonstration Exercises _____

1. b.
2. c.
3. d.
4. d.
5. a.
6. b.
7. b.
8. a.
9. c.
10. d.

SYNOPSIS OF *READINGS IN MANAGEMENT ACCOUNTING* AND QUESTIONS TO ASSIGN WITH SUGGESTED ANSWERS

Synopsis of Readings in Management Accounting

Four articles on activity-based costing are included in this section. Taken together, the articles highlight the applications of ABC to many different types of organizations.

The first (Reading 7.1) is a good introductory overview of activity-based costing (ABC) by Terence Pare, "A New Tool for Managing Costs." Apart from discussing concerns related to traditional costing systems, the article focuses on companies that have successfully implemented ABC such as Dana Corporation, an automobile parts maker; Advanced Micro Devices, producer of semiconductors; and Chrysler Corporation. Chrysler, for instance, had a lot of success in using ABC to determine the optimal number of wire harnesses for their new minivans. Nine departments agreed to participate in the process. An ABC analysis showed that the optimal number of harnesses was two. Since everyone agreed that two was the correct number, an added bonus was the reduction in political fighting across the various departments.

While the early applications of ABC were developed in manufacturing settings, more recent applications have surfaced in service organizations. William Rotch's article, Reading 7.2, "Activity-Based Costing in Service Organizations," addresses two questions relating to whether ABC can be adapted for use in service organizations, and if so, whether there are special considerations that need to be made. Citing examples from a hospital, rail services, and data analysis organizations, Rotch believes that services can quite easily adapt ABC. Services do differ from manufacturing in that output is harder to define, and there are some difficult issues such as joint capacity costs to deal with, but these are not insurmountable problems. In fact the last two articles in the section, David Carlson and Mark Young's "Activity-Based Total Quality Management at American Express," (Reading 7.3) and Lawrence Carr's "Unbundling the Cost of Hospitalization," (Reading 7.4) provide examples of how ABC can be applied in other service settings.

Synopsis of Readings in Management Accounting

Carlson and Young studied a division of American Express, American Express Integrated Payment Systems (now called First Data Corporation). The article documents the FACT (Functional Administrative Control Technique) approach for combining activity-based costing, strategic cost management and total quality management. Developed by Brian Higgins, director of quality assurance, the system has a feature that distinguishes it from many other systems. Apart from a regular activity hierarchy, Higgins' model incorporates nonfinancial information such as customer and supplier comments into the data base and, ultimately into decision making. Apart from its intuitive appeal FACT saved Integrated Payments Systems over a $1 million dollars during the first year of operation.

Reading 7.4, "Unbundling the Cost of Hospitalization," by Lawrence Carr, illustrates the implementation of an ABC system at Braintree Hospital in Boston. This application was designed to tease apart (or unbundle) the fixed cost allocation of nursing services. In the past, nursing costs were simply allocated into the cost per day of a hospital room. However, since nurses have different professional qualifications and skills, and patients require different care and have differential lengths of stay, devising a more accurate costing system would be beneficial to patients and the hospital. Certainly a patient would no longer be charged the average cost of nursing, especially if he or she required little nursing care, and the hospital would have a much more diagnostic system for activity and cost control.

Points to Include in Answering Questions from the Readings

1. In Pare's article, why does Robert Kaplan, one of the developers of ABC, state that he would take the term "cost" out of activity-based costing if he could do it over again?

    Students answers should include:
    a. Some critics have said that ABC focuses too narrowly on costs and that some future benefits can be missed.
    b. Kaplan believes that ABC is "power for strategic management."

2. Rotch cites examples of outputs in service organizations. List three of these. Do you think that they are different from outputs in manufacturing organizations? Why?

    Students answers should include:
    a. speed of service, quality of information, and satisfaction provided.
    b. Since most of these benefits can be quantified in dollar terms, in many ways the problems are the same. The difficulty lies in the procedure for quantification (e.g. developing scales for customer satisfaction and then tying these to dollar amounts).

Points to Include in Answering Questions from the Readings

3.   What are the four "cost of quality" categories listed in the Carlson and Young article. Why are the categories important?

Student answers should include:
a.   prevention
b.   appraisal.
c.   internal failure.
d.   external failure.

The distinctions among these concepts are important as each refers to very specific types of quality problems. For example external failure costs arise when a product failures in the hands of the customer. Correcting such a problem is not only costly because company representatives have to go to the site, but also customers are usually very annoyed and this can reduce repeat business. An article by Simpson and Muthler in Chapter 9 "Quality Costs Facilitating the Quality Initiative" discusses these issues more fully.

4.   In Lawrence Carr's article on the cost of healthcare, the consumption of nursing services is a function of what factors?

Student answers should include:
a.   the mix of patient diagnosis such as stroke, spinal cord injury, fractures, joint replacement, burns, etc.
b.   length of hospital stay or the number of patient days in the hospital

An analysis of these factors, taken together, led to the ABC model.

Recommended Cases

1.   Seligram, Inc.: Electronic Testing Operations is an excellent case on two-stage allocations (HBS case 189-084 and teaching note 9-189-084).

2.   Mayers Tap, Inc. (A), (B) and (C) are an excellent series of cases related to the design of costing systems.   This series relies on some spreadsheet work for students.   If you use this series be sure that you obtain the most recent version of the disks so that they are compatible with the latest version of LOTUS 2.01 or above (9-088-001).   HBS cases 185-111 (A, B and C), software module 5-185-069, and video teaching guide is also available 9-885-501

3.   Destin Brass is a very good introductory case on ABC. (HBS case 190-089) and teaching note 5-191-029.

Chapter 8

Pricing and Product Mix Decisions

CENTRAL FOCUS AND LEARNING OBJECTIVES

This chapter introduces a number of issues relating to pricing and product mix considerations including:

1. How a firm chooses its product mix in the short run in response to prices set in the market for its products

2. How a firm adjusts its prices in the short run depending on whether capacity is limited

3. How a firm determines a long-run benchmark price to guide its pricing strategy

4. How a firm evaluates the long-run profitability of its products and market segments

Chapter Overview

A number of central issues relating to product mix and pricing decisions are addressed in Chapter 8. Discussion begins with definitions of price taking and price setting. A price taker is a firm that has little or no influence on an industry's supply and demand forces and hence the prices of its products. Price setters, on the other hand, usually enjoy a significant market share and can set the prices of their products.

Four different situations are considered in the chapter based on whether a decision is short- or long-run in nature and whether the firm is a price taker or price setter. A number of other important concepts are introduced including, incremental costs and revenues, marginal cost and revenue and opportunity costs. Finally markup strategies such as penetration pricing and skimming pricing are discussed.

Chapter Outline _____

 The material in this chapter together with the readings should address a number of issues for managers of all types. However, students concentrating in marketing and strategy should find this chapter of particular interest. You may want to mention this to increase involvement.

Learning Objective 1: The way a firm chooses its product mix in the short-term in response to prices set in the market for its products. DO MULTIPLE CHOICE QUESTIONS 1, 2 and 3.

I.   Role of Product Costs in Pricing and Product Mix Decisions

    A.   Understanding how product costs should be analyzed is extremely important for both **pricing decisions**.

    B.   If prices are set by market forces, the firm has to decide on the **product mix** to produce and sell.

II.   Short and Long-Run Pricing Decisions

    A.   Many resources committed to activities are more than likely fixed in the short-run as capacities cannot be easily altered.

    B.   In the short-run, special attention must be paid to the time period over which capacity is committed, as commitments may constrain the firm and not allow it to seek more profitable opportunities.

    C.   If production is constrained by inadequate capacity, overtime or the use of subcontractors may be necessary.

    D.   In the long-run, managers have more flexibility in adjusting the capacities of activity resources to match demand for resources.

E.   Whether the firm can influence market prices is also important. There are two general types of firms, price-takers and price-setters.

    1.   A **Price-taker firm** is one that has little or no influence on the industry supply and demand forces, and, consequently, on the prices of its products.

    2.   A **Price-setter firm** is one that sets or bids the prices of its products because it enjoys a significant market share in its industry segment.

III.   Short-Run Product Mix Decisions

A.   Small firms who are price-takers can have little influence on the overall industry supply and demand and thus influence on the prices of its products. Small firms cannot demand a higher price for their products as customers may go elsewhere, and if the firm tries to lower prices below industry prices, large firms might retaliate by engaging in a price war which would make the small firm and the industry worse off.

B.   The simple decision rule for a price-taker firm is *to sell as many of its products as possible as long as their costs are less than their prices.* But two considerations must be kept in mind:

    1.   What costs are **relevant** to the short-run product mix decision? Should all product costs be included or only those that vary in the short-run?

    2.   Managers may not be able to produce and sell more of those products whose costs are less than their prices given capacity constraints. In other words, how **flexible** are the capacities of the firm's activity resources?

 Exhibits 8-2 through 8-7 on the Texcel Company provide a comprehensive example of short-run product mix decisions.

3. The Texcel example illustrates a key point and that is the criterion on which to decide which products are the most profitable to produce and sell at prevailing prices is contingent on the **contribution margin per unit of the constrained resource** (which was machine hours in this example).

IV. The Impact of Opportunity Costs

A variation in the Texcel problem discussed above is to consider a situation in which a decision-maker makes a choice of one alternative over another. Thus, an opportunity cost arises.

A. An **opportunity cost,** is the potential benefit sacrificed when, in selecting one alternative, another alternative is given up.

B. The decision rule for deciding between two alternatives in an opportunity cost situation is to make the decision which **minimizes the opportunity cost.** Thus, the product that has the **lowest contribution margin per unit of constrained resource** should be sacrificed.

Learning Objective 2: The way a firm adjusts its prices in the short-term depending on whether capacity is limited. DO MULTIPLE CHOICE QUESTIONS 4, 5 and 6.

V. Short-Run Pricing Decisions

A. This section discusses the relationship between costs and prices bid by a supplier for special orders that do not involve long-term relationships with the customer. Two cases are discussed when there is available surplus capacity and no available surplus capacity.

 Review the Chaney Tools and Dies Company example in Exhibit 8-8. Full costs are the sum of all costs (direct materials, direct labor and overhead) assigned to a product.

1.   Available Surplus Capacity

   a.   When capacity is available, incremental revenues have to be greater than incremental costs.

   b.   **Incremental costs** (or revenues) are the amount by which costs (or revenues) change if one particular decision is made instead of another.

   c.   **Incremental cost per unit** is the amount by which total production costs and sales increase when one additional unit of a product is produced and sold.

2.   No Available Surplus Capacity

   a.   When there is no available capacity, a firm will have to incur costs to acquire the necessary capacity. This may mean operating the plant on an overtime basis.

   b.   Again, the decision rule is that incremental revenues will have to greater than incremental costs.

B.   **Another key term is relevant costs** (and revenues). These are the costs (revenues) that differ across alternatives and therefore, must be considered in deciding which alternative is the best. Incremental costs are the relevant costs for the kinds of short-run decisions discussed above.

Readings in Management Accounting

Bruce Committe and Jacque Grinnell's "Predatory Pricing, the Price-Cost Test, and Activity-Based Costing," (Reading 8.1) provides some legal background to an important issue in pricing - the price-cost test.

Ask students to review the elements of short-run pricing and mix decisions

Learning Objective 3: The way a firm determines a long-term benchmark price to guide its pricing strategy. DO MULTIPLE CHOICE QUESTIONS 7 and 8.

VI.   Long-Run Pricing Decisions

A.   Relevant costs for short-run special order pricing decisions differ from full costs. What is the benefit of having full cost information?

B.   Reliance on full costs for pricing can be justified in three types of situations:

1.   Government contacts and contracts with electric utilities and others that specify prices as full costs with a markup.

2.   A long-term contract allows for greater flexibility in adjusting the level of commitment for all activity resources. Thus, since most activity costs will depend on the production decisions under the long-term contract, full costs are relevant for the long-run pricing decision.

3.   Because of short-run fluctuations based on demand for products, firms adjust their prices up and down over a period of time. Over the long-run, their average prices tend to equal the price based on full costs that may be set in a long-term contract.

C.   The amount of markup is contingent on several factors:

1.   If the **strength of demand** for the product is high a higher markup can be used.

2. If **demand is elastic**, a small increase in price results in a large decrease in demand. Markups are lower when demand is elastic.

3. When competition is intense markups decrease as it is hard for firms to sustain prices much higher than their incremental costs.

4. Markups may be purposefully lowered based on firm strategy. Two types of strategies are:

    a. A **skimming price strategy** which involves charging a higher price initially from customers willing to pay more for the privilege of possessing a new product.

    b. A **penetration pricing strategy** which is charging a lower price initially to win over market share from an established product of a competing firm.

Readings in Management Accounting

Thomas Dudick's "Pricing Strategies for Manufacturers," (Reading 8. 2) suggests factors that should be considered for common pricing strategies such as premium and marginal pricing.

Learning Objective 4: The way a firm evaluates the long-term profitability of its products and market segments. DO MULTIPLE CHOICE QUESTIONS 9 and 10.

VII. Long-Run Mix Decisions

A. Decisions to add new, or drop existing products from the product portfolio, often have long-term implications for the cost structure of the firm.

B.   Resources committed for batch-related and product-sustaining activities cannot be easily changed in the short-run, so changing the mix cannot be done quickly.

C.   Another consideration is that, in some cases, customer may desire a firm to maintain a full product line so that they do not have to go elsewhere. Thus, some unprofitable products may have be kept to maintain the entire product line. If this is too costly, managers might try methods such as reengineering to lower the cost of some products.

D.   One caveat is that dropping products will only help profitability if managers also eliminate, or redeploy the activity resources no longer required to support the dropped product.

 Ask students to review the key features of long-term pricing and mix decisions.

Readings in Management Accounting

Ronald Lewis' "Activity-Based Costing for Marketing," (Reading 8.2) presents a good link between marketing costs and activity-based costing.

VIII.   Appendix 8A

A.   The focus of the Appendix is to present an economic analysis of the pricing decision. Note that a knowledge of basic differential calculus is need to work through the examples.

B.   The quantity choice is examined and presented in terms of equating marginal revenue and marginal cost. **Marginal revenues** are the increase in revenues (or costs) for a unit increase in the quantity produced and sold.

 Review the examples and study the graphs in Exhibits 8A.1 through 8A.4.

Below is an exercise in pricing that you may wish to try to increase student understanding and involvement of pricing in competitive settings. If you have any questions regarding procedures please get in touch with Professor Rajiv Banker at the University of Minnesota.

A PRICING EXPERIMENT

(Rajiv D. Banker and P. Jane Saly)

The objective of this experiment is to introduce students to pricing decisions in a competitive setting. Its two principal learning objectives are:

(1) Expectations about competitors' pricing decisions must enter a firm's own pricing decisions.

(2) The type of cost accounting system used (single driver or multiple driver) influences the equilibrium prices in the industry.

The instructor should provide *one* of the following two confidential cost reports to each team. All teams in one industry may be provided the cost report based on a single cost driver system, and all teams in another industry may be provided the cost report based on a multiple cost driver system.

Single Cost Driver System:

INDUSTRY_____	FIRM_____

Cost Estimates - Private Information

Your accountant has looked at all the costs incurred for your firm and come up with the following **confidential** information:

Direct material costs are $8.00 per pair of Lightweight Boots and $20.00 per pair of Mountaineering Boots.

Direct labor requirements are 0.5 hours per pair of Lightweight Boots and 1 hour per pair of Mountaineering Boots. Direct labor wage rate (inclusive of benefits) is $8.00 per hour.

Overhead costs are applied to products at the rate of $14.00 per machine hour. Each pair of Lightweight and Mountaineering Boots requires 0.8 machine hours.

While these are all the costs of producing and selling these products, they are only **estimates**. Actual costs will differ somewhat. Remember to keep your costs secret!

Multiple Cost Driver System:

INDUSTRY_____	FIRM_____

Cost Estimates - Private Information

Your accountant has looked at all the costs incurred for your firm and come up with the following **confidential** information:

Direct material costs are $8.00 per pair of Lightweight Boots and $20.00 per pair of Mountaineering Boots.

Direct labor requirements are 0.5 hours per pair of Lightweight Boots and 1 hour per pair of Mountaineering Boots. Direct labor wage rate (inclusive of benefits) is $8.00 per hour.

There are two overhead cost pools corresponding to two cost drivers (machine hours and number of setups). Overhead is applied to products at the rate of $5.00 per machine hour and $600 per setup. Lightweight Boots are manufactured in batches of 150 pairs; each batch requires a total of 120 machine hours. Mountaineering Boots are manufactured in batches of 30 pairs; each batch requires a total of 24 machine hours.

While these are all the costs of producing and selling these products, they are only **estimates**. Actual costs will differ somewhat. Remember to keep your costs secret!

Solution:

Estimates of the variable costs (v) of the two products depend on whether the team is provided data from a single cost driver or a multiple cost driver system:

	Single Cost Driver		Multiple Cost Driver	
	LT	MT	LT	MT
Direct Material	$ 8.00	$ 20.00	$8.00	$ 20.00
Direct Labor	4.00	8.00	4.00	8.00
Overhead - Machine hours	11.20	11.20	4.00	4.00
Overhead - Setup			4.00	20.00
Total variable cost	$ 23.20	$39.20	$20.00	$52.00

The contribution, Π, from either product is represented by the following expression:

$$\Pi = (P - v) Q$$

$$= (P - v) (a - bP + e(P_1 + P_2 + P_3))$$

where a, b, and e are the parameters in the appropriate demand function $Q = a - bP + e(P_1 + P_2 + P_3)$. Suppose $\overline{P} = (P_1 + P_2 + P_3)/3$ is the average price expected to be set by the three competing firms. Then,

$$\Pi = (P - v) (a - bP + 3e\overline{P})$$

Profit maximization requires

$$d\Pi/dP = a - 2bP + 3e\overline{P} + vb = 0.$$

Therefore, the profit maximizing price, P^0, given average competitor price, $\overline{P}$, is:

$$P^0 = (a + vb + 3e\overline{P})/2b$$

If, however, we assume that all firms in the industry are identical and $\overline{P} = P^0$ then the equilibrium price, P^*, can be determined using the following expression

$$P^* = \frac{a + vb}{2b - 3e}$$

The logic underlying this expression is similar to that described in Appendix 8.1. Contribution to profit at equilibrium prices is determined as

$$\text{Contribution} = (P^* - v) Q^*$$

where $Q^* = a - bP^* + 3eP^*$ (because there are 3 other identical competing firms) is the demand quantity at equilibrium prices, and is obtained by inserting the value P^* in the appropriate demand function.

The numerical solutions for equilibrium prices and contribution to profit for the two products are as follows:

Single Cost Driver Industry

	Equilibrium Prices	Estimated Contribution	True Contribution
Product LT	$ 42	$ 178,656	$ 209,066
Product MT	66	80,453	43,540
		$ 259,109	$ 252,606

Multiple Cost Driver Industry

	Equilibrium Prices	Estimated Contribution	True Contribution
Product LT	$ 40	$ 199,980	$ 199,980
Product MT	75	57,661	57,661
		$ 257,641	$ 257,641

You will find that the industry prices converge by the fifth period to price levels close to (but not necessarily the same as) the equilibrium prices. In the single cost driver case, the product MT is undercosted and LT is overcosted; their equilibrium prices reflect these cost distortions. Notice that there is no variance between estimated and true contribution (and between estimated and actual net income, reported to all teams in each period) for multiple cost driver firms, but there is a variance of $6,503 ($259,109 - $252,606) for single cost driver firms.

In this case, the true firm profits are *lower* when all firms in the industry use a single cost driver system than when they all use a multiple cost driver system ($252,606 versus $257,641). This illustrates that even in a competitive setting, more accurate cost information may make you better off. However, this is *not* always true. It is possible that for certain values of the cost and demand parameters, the equilibrium prices in a single cost driver industry result in *higher* profits than in a multiple cost driver industry. See, Rajiv D. Banker and Gordon Potter, "Economic Evaluation of Single Cost Driver Systems," *Journal of Management Accounting Research*, Fall 1993, pp. 15-32.

Chapter Quiz/Demonstration Exercises _____

1. The key difference between firms who are price setters and those who are price takers is:

    (a) price setting firms usually have greater total assets than price taking firms.
    (b) price setting firms have a much higher contribution margin than price taking firms and are thus have more influence on prices.
    (c) price setting firms have a strong influence over industry supply and demand forces and price taking firms do not.
    (d) price setting firms have less long-term debt than price taking firms.

2. Small firms in industries such as automobile parts manufacturing, steel, and generic chemicals usually:

    (a) are price setters.
    (b) can influence prices.
    (c) are price makers.
    (d) are price takers.

(3) When faced with making a decision of which products to produce and sell at current prices, the most important decision criterion is:

    (a) the contribution margin per unit.
    (b) the contribution margin per unit of constrained resource.
    (c) overall profit margin per unit.
    (d) the overall profit margin per unit of constrained resource.

4. Each of the factors below influences short-run pricing decisions, EXCEPT:

    (a) the level of facility-sustaining activities and costs.
    (c) the time period of the contract over which capacity is committed.
    (b) whether surplus capacity is available for additional production.
    (d) whether the available capacity limits production.

5. Of the two products that Webber Company produces, Web1 has a contribution per unit of $4.00 and requires .33 machine hours

per unit, while Web2 has a contribution of $2.65 and requires .22 machine hours per unit. Webber's policy is to only sell products with a contribution per unit of constrained resource greater than $12.10. What Webber Company do?

(a)   Sell both Web1 and Web2.
(b)   Sell only Web1.
(c)   Sell only Web2.
(d)   Sell neither Web 1 nor Web2.

6.   Under each of the following circumstances, full cost pricing can be economically justified, EXCEPT:

(b)   when contracts are developed with governmental agencies.
(a)   when customized products are manufactured.
(c)   when a firm enters into a short-term contractual relationship with a customer to supply a product.
(d)   when a firm enters into a long-term contractual relationship with a customer to supply a product.

7.   When a firm uses a low markup for a new product is using a:

(a)   full-cost pricing strategy.
(b)   opportunity pricing strategy.
(c)   skimming pricing strategy.
(d)   penetration pricing strategy.

8.   The term elasticity of demand means:

(a)   a small increase in price results in a large decrease in demand.
(b)   a small increase in price results in a small decrease in demand.
(b)   a price increase causes demand to fluctuate wildly.
(d)   a price increase causes demand to increase.

9.   The decision to drop a major product line that is produced in large batches will likely affect which kinds of costs?

(a)   Unit-related costs only.
(b)   Unit-related and batch-related costs only.
(c)   Batch-related costs only.
(d)   Unit-related, batch-related and product-sustaining costs.

10.   Of the strategies below for reducing the cost of a product which will probably be the least effective?

(a)   Provide quantity discounts for customers to increase their order sizes.
(b)   Reengineer the product
(c)   Decrease the functionality of the product.
(d)   Differentiate their products further so that prices can be raised and costs brought more in line with prices.

Solutions to Chapter Quiz/Demonstration Exercises _____

1. c.
2. d.
3. b.
4. a.
5. b.
6. c.
7. d.
8. a.
9. d.
10. c.

SYNOPSIS OF *READINGS IN MANAGEMENT ACCOUNTING* AND QUESTIONS TO ASSIGN WITH SUGGESTED ANSWERS

Synopsis of Readings in Management Accounting

Reading 8.1 is Bruce Committe and D. Jacque Grinnell's *"Predatory Pricing, the Price-Cost Test, and Activity-Based Costing,"* which describes the issue of predatory pricing. Predatory pricing occurs when firms price their products and services in such a way that competition is driven out and service price barriers to entry are created for new market entrants. Antitrust legislation has deemed this practice unlawful since it can often result in monopolies. The authors discuss the four major U.S. antitrust statutes which helped form the foundation for legislation on predatory pricing and ultimately the price-cost test. Currently this test involves determining whether a company's prices fall below the short-run average variable cost. While this is not universally accepted, prices below this level are considered predatory. Committe and Grinnell argue that activity-based costing can provide more guidance in determining the appropriate cost and suggest that long-run incremental costs be used as the cost basis.

In *"Pricing Strategies for Manufacturers"* (Reading 8.2), Thomas Dudick suggests close scrutiny of each company's pricing strategy to ensure that it is being implemented appropriately and offers sound prescriptive advice on a variety of pricing topics. For example, Dudick argues that companies following a premium pricing strategy often simply add a fixed dollar amount for their deluxe models, rather than a predetermined profit percentage. In many cases the fixed dollar amount results in a lower percentage return than on standard models, thereby shortchanging the bottom line. Other topics discussed include marginal pricing as an appropriate strategy when a firm has developed a cost advantage over its competitors pricing new products, in pricing replacement parts, and cost-based pricing.

Synopsis of Readings in Management Accounting

Ronald Lewis' piece, *"Activity-Based Costing for Marketing"* (Reading 8.3), focuses on the problem of how to account for marketing costs, and in particular, distribution costs. Since marketing costs constitute more than 50% of the total costs in many product lines, not considering them appropriately can result in inaccurate product costing and pricing. Using data from the Atlanta Company, Lewis develops an activity-based costing approach to handling marketing costs. Cost drivers for activities such as selling, advertising, warehousing, packing and shipping, and general office are developed and costs are assigned accordingly. Analysis can then be undertaken by product, sales territory and product line.

Points to Include in Answering Questions from the Readings

1.   According to Committe and Grinnell, what is the price-cost test, and why is it important?

Student answers should include:
a.   Passing the price-cost test means that a company is selling its products or services above their short run average cost.
b.   This is important in order to prevent some firms from trying to gain monopoly positions in an industry.

2.   What is the role of intuition when making pricing decisions, according to Dudick?

Student answers should include:
a.   There is a role of intuition in pricing decisions but "only after the appropriate pricing strategy is applied and the results evaluated carefully."
b.   As an illustration of this, see Dudick premium pricing example.

Points to Include in Answering Questions from the Readings

3.   In Lewis' article, what are the appropriate cost drivers for selling, advertising, warehousing, packing and shipping, and general office activities?

Student answers should include:

Marketing Activity	Cost Driver
a. Selling	Dollar value of sales
b. Advertising	Quantity of units sold
c. Warehousing	Weight of items shipped
d. Packing and shipping	Quantity of items shipped
e. General office	Number of customers' orders

Recommended Cases

1.   Madison Clock (A) and (B) in Rotch's et al.'s casebook can be used here. This case was also suggested for Chapter 4, so if you didn't do it then, it can apply to this chapter as well.

2.   Hanson Manufacturing (HBS case 9-156-004) focuses on pricing strategy.

3.   Destin Brass (HBS 9-191-029; teaching note 5-191-029) deals with pricing within an activity-based costing framework. This case was also recommended for Chapter 7.

Chapter 9

Process and Activity Decisions

CENTRAL FOCUS AND LEARNING OBJECTIVES

Chapter 9 looks at many factors related to process and activity decisions including:

1. The reason why sunk costs are not relevant costs

2. The analysis required to decide whether to make or buy components for a product

3. The way in which qualitative factors influence the quantitative analysis of such decisions

4. The reasons why reductions in inventories especially work-in-process inventories, and reduction in production cycle time result in cost savings

5. The way that improvements in production yields and reductions in rework and defect rates result in cost savings

Chapter Overview _____

A number of central ideas on decision making with management accounting information are presented in this chapter. These include determining which costs are sunk, which are avoidable, which are relevant and the role of qualitative factors in decision making. These concepts are illustrated within the context of the make-buy decision.

The relationships among process choices, activities and costs also are presented. The topics discussed include how cellular manufacturing reduces cycle time and inventory, and in turn, how reductions in inventory reduce costs. Cost savings can also be realized by improving in production yields and defect rates, and reducing rework.

Chapter Outline _____

> The material in this chapter integrates well with similar topics presented in an operations management course. Stress again to students that the study of management accounting ties to many aspects of the business curriculum.

Learning Objective 1: The reasons that sunk costs are not relevant costs. DO MULTIPLE CHOICE QUESTION 1.

I.   Evaluation of Monetary Decisions and Relevant Costs

> This section discusses the monetary implications of decisions and the appropriate tradeoffs between costs and benefits resulting from different alternatives. The key question is which costs are relevant for decisions?

A.   **Sunk costs** are costs of resources that have already been committed, and regardless of what decision is made by managers, these costs cannot be avoided. *Sunk costs are not considered relevant costs.*

> Review the Milanca Company example on relevant costs for the decision to purchase a new machine. Note that the purchase price of the old machine and the payments that must be made on it are sunk costs and not relevant for the decision. Further, Exhibit 9-2 illustrates that the relevant cash outflows and inflows.

Learning Objective 2: The analysis required to decide whether to make or buy components for a product. DO MULTIPLE CHOICE QUESTIONS 2 and 3.

II.   Make or Buy Decisions

    A.   The **make or buy decision** is to either make a part or component in-house or source it from an outside supplier.

        1.   **Outsourcing** is purchasing a product, part or component from an outside supplier instead of manufacturing it in-house

        2.   **Avoidable costs** are those that are eliminated when a part, a product, a product line, or a business segment is discontinued.

Learning Objective 3: The way in which qualitative factors influence the quantitative analysis of such decisions. DO MULTIPLE CHOICE QUESTIONS 4.

        3.   **Qualitative factors** such as the reputation of a supplier, can help influence quantitative decisions. Factors such as the supplier's ability to meet performance standards on time are critical to success. Some businesses have chosen to certify suppliers. A **certified supplier** is a specially selected supplier who is assured a high level of business for conforming to high standards for quality and delivery schedules

 Review Exhibit 9-3 on the make-or-buy decision.

Learning Objective 4: The reasons that reductions in inventories, especially work-in-process inventories, and reduction in production cycle time result in cost savings. DO MULTIPLE CHOICE QUESTIONS 5, 6, 7 and 8.

Readings in Management Accounting

Reading 9.1 by A. Faye Borthick and Harold Roth, "Accounting for Time: Reengineering Business Processes to Improve Responsiveness," presents a good overview of time-based competition.

III.   Reduction in Cycle Time and Inventory

     A.   **Production cycle time** is the time elapsed beginning with the receipt of raw materials and ending with the shipment of the final product

     B.   **Cellular manufacturing** is a way of organizing the plant into a number of cells, so that within each cell, all machines required for the manufacture of a group of similar products are arranged sequentially in close proximity to each other.

Review Exhibits 9-4 through 9-8 on Treadwell Electric Corporation. In Exhibit 9-8, in particular note the cost savings from reducing the financing investment in work-in-process inventory. This is a critical savings.

     C.   Often **plant reorganization** can result in increased sales because of decreases in cycle time and reduction in inventory-related costs because of the decrease in work-in-process inventory.

Review the dialogue between Karen Leonard and the production and sales managers. Interviews of this sort are extremely important to gather the necessary information to make informed decisions.

Readings in Management Accounting

Michael D. Shields and S. Mark Young's "Effective Long-Term Cost Reduction: A Strategic Perspective," (Reading 9. 2) focuses on tying cost reduction to strategy and cautions against blindly eliminating people to reduce costs.

Learning Objective 5: The way that improvements in production yields and reductions in rework and defect rates result in cost savings. DO MULTIPLE CHOICE QUESTIONS 9 and 10.

Readings in Management Accounting

James Simpson and David Muthler, "Quality Costs: Facilitating the Quality Initiative," (Reading 9.3) develops the four areas of cost of quality in some depth. The reading fits in well with process and activity decision making.

IV.   Improvements in Production Yield

The Jorgenson Jewelry Products example illustrates how a company improved on a number of variables such as decreasing rework and reducing cycle time. Paul Petersen studied the following variables and steps in analyzing the situation.

A.   Production flows -- Note the flowchart in Exhibit 9-9.

B.   Work-in-Process Inventory.

C.   Production Costs -- See Exhibit 9-10.

D.   Cost of Rework. **Rework** consists of production activities required to bring defective units up to minimum quality standards. See Exhibit 9-11.

E.   Carrying Work-in-Process Inventory.

F.   Increased Sales -- See Exhibit 9-12.

G.   Summary of Benefits -- Exhibit 9-13 summarizes the annual benefits from the Quality Improvement Program.

Review Exhibits 9-9 to 9-13. Understanding the process that Paul Petersen went through will provide more insight into how quality improvements can be made.

Chapter Quiz/Demonstration Exercises _____

1. The one principle that is applicable about sunk costs in all situations is that sunk costs are:

    (a) are only relevant for decisions involving replacing old machinery.
    (b) not relevant costs.
    (c) those that can be avoided.
    (d) are relevant costs.

2. Jimmy Young's Company, Hong Kong Associates, has collected the following information related to a decision to purchase a new machine and dispose of their old machine: The book value of the old machine is $11,000, the disposal value of the old machine is $25,000, the cost savings in maintenance by purchasing the new machine is $4,500, and the down payment on the new machine is $13,000. What is the sum of the relevant cost savings and cash inflows?

    (a) $40,500
    (b) $53,500
    (c) $4,500
    (d) $29,500

3. When a product or component is purchased from an outside supplier rather than making it in-house _____ has occurred.

    (a) process improvement.
    (b) rework.
    (c) outsourcing.
    (d) cellular manufacturing.

4. A certified supplier usually meets each of the following criteria, EXCEPT

    (a) The supplier must operate on a just-in-time basis.
    (b) The supplier must have a strong reputation for service.
    (c) The supplier must meet delivery schedules.
    (d) The supplier must have high quality standards.

5. Bonner Company has recorded the following data regarding its inventories. To manufacture product B35, it takes 1 hour to move raw materials to the work-in-process area. Transforming the raw materials into finished goods takes three production steps of 4 hours each. The finished goods are then temporarily stored in a storage area of 12 hours until they are shipped to the customer. It takes 14 hours for customers to receive the shipment. What is the total cycle time of B35?

   (a)   27 hours.
   (b)   39 hours.
   (c)   13 hours.
   (d)   25 hours.

6. Implementing a cellular manufacturing layout, usually incurs the following kinds of costs, EXCEPT:

   (a)   the cost of new benefits for workers.
   (b)   the costs of training the workers.
   (c)   the cost of reinstallation of the machines.
   (d)   the cost of moving machines.

7. Which of the following does not result in reductions in the level of work-in-process inventory and cycle time?

   (a)   Cellular manufacturing.
   (b)   Quality improvement programs.
   (c)   Adding more functions to an existing product.
   (d)   Corporate rightsizing programs.

8. Wilder Company has capacity to produce 4000 units of product YF74. Currently it is producing 3200 units. Brooks Company asks Wilder to produce 650 more units of YF74 as a special favor. Neither new machinery nor extra plant space is needed for the special order. Which of the following statements is true?

   (a)   Neither product-sustaining nor facility sustaining costs will increase.
   (b)   Only facility-sustaining costs will increase.
   (c)   Only product-sustaining costs will increase.
   (d)   Both product-sustaining and facility-sustaining costs will increase.

9. Typically, if work-in-process is reduced, which of the following statements is false:

(a) the cost of financing inventory decreases.
(b) the cost of materials handling labor decreases.
(c) the cost of materials scrap and obsolescence decreases.
(d) the cost of factory floor space per square foot decreases.

10. In correcting a major defect in a batch of 50 class rings, which of the following is true?

(a) Both batch related and product-sustaining overhead costs would increase.
(b) Both unit-related and batch-related overhead costs would increase.
(c) Only unit-related overhead costs would increase.
(d) Only facility-sustaining overhead costs would increase.

Solutions to Chapter Quiz/Demonstration Exercises _____

1. b.
2. d.
3. c.
4. a.
5. b.
6. a.
7. c.
8. a.
9. d.
10. b.

Synopsis of Readings in Management Accounting

The readings in this section all relate to various aspects of process and activity decisions. A. Faye Borthick and Harold Roth's "*Accounting for Time: Reengineering Business Processes to Improve Responsiveness*" (Reading 9.1) discusses how the concept of time must be considered in all process decisions. Many companies compete now on time-based variables such as speed to market and cycle time. A goal of many of these firms is to significantly reduce "noncontributing time" (or non-value added time), or the amount of time in the total product or service life cycle that can be eliminated without diminishing the value of products or services. Techniques for reducing noncontributing time include eliminating redundant activities, decreasing the time it takes to perform activities, and coordinating deliveries in order all parts of an order arrive simultaneously so that customers do not have to wait for one part of an order. Activity-based costing is recommended for identifying activities and developing costs for each activity.

Another process that is critical for many firms is reducing costs without adversely affecting the mission and objectives of an organization. In "*Effective Long-Term Cost Reduction: A Strategic Perspective*" (Reading 9.2), by Michael D. Shields and S. Mark Young, the authors caution against the most expedient, short-term, traditional method for reducing costs -- firing employees. This traditional approach has a number of significant ramifications such as reducing employee morale and motivation and losing valuable work-related knowledge as each employee is let go. Both morale and motivation decline as remaining employees experience greater stress as they have more work to do, and many worry that they will be next. In turn, coordination problems such as production delays, missed schedules, and decreases in quality and delivery time can occur. Shields and Young argue for a much more strategic approach to cost reduction and develop a set of guidelines that firms can use to avoid the "slash and burn" traditional approach. These guidelines focus on reducing costs by improving organizational activities and processes and viewing employees as resources rather than as costs.

Synopsis of Readings in Management Accounting

Building primarily on the work of J. M. Juran, James Simpson and David Muthler's "*Quality Costs: Facilitating the Quality Initiative*" (Reading 9.3) illustrates a framework for understanding the cost-of-quality. The framework includes four areas in the cost-of-quality: external failure costs (when a product fails in the hands of the customer), internal failure costs (scrap, rework, downtime caused by defects, etc.), appraisal costs (inspections, quality audits, etc.), and prevention costs (quality engineering, quality training, etc.). Once quality costs are categorized they can be quantified in dollar terms. The area of determining the cost of quality is highly significant; research indicates that poor quality can cost a company 10 to 20% of its sales revenue. Simpson and Muthler suggest ways to create and implement an effective quality cost program.

Points to Include in Answering Questions from the Readings

1. What are the reasons for so much noncontributing time in many organizations?

    Student answers should include:
    a. The need to be more responsive has only recently become critical given global and national competition.
    b. The tradition of focusing solely on cost is deeply entrenched and separating cost and time issues is still a fairly new concept.
    c. Product costing has traditionally focused on manufacturing cost and ignored many support and administrative functions which is also where noncontributing time can exist.
    d. Time-based thinking requires cooperation from many people and groups who have traditionally not worked together.
    e. Information systems to help reduce noncontributing time are expensive.
    f. Potential changes in the nature of work and new working relationships make people resistant to change.

Points to Include in Answering Questions from the Readings

2. What are five of the most frequently used traditional cost reduction programs, and how effective is each one?

Student answers should include:

a. The technology approach focuses on replacing labor with technology. Not very effective especially given that labor content in product costs is decreasing.

b. The lean and mean approach uses across the board cuts through layoff and reductions in pay and benefits. Not very effective, especially in the long run as the amount of work stays the same or increases and the workforce is smaller. Ultimately morale and motivation problems can take over.

c. Offshore retreat can reduce costs, but to a large extent the effectiveness depends on how employees at home are treated. Morale problems can be significant with this approach.

d. Mergers can create economies of scale by eliminating overlapping employees, products, plants and overhead. But problems can often occur in assimilating diverse or incompatible management styles, corporate cultures, product lines, etc.

e. Diversification into new industries in the hope of finding a less expensive operating environment can sometimes be effective, but a key concern is whether the firm is expanding beyond its core competency. Costs can increase dramatically as the firm ventures into new products and technologies.

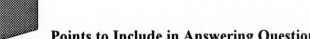

Points to Include in Answering Questions from the Readings

3.   What are the four cost-of-quality areas? Specify three types of costs within each category.

Student answers should include:
a.   External failure
-      warranty adjustments
-      product recalls
-      product liability suits
b.   Internal Failure costs
-      rework
-      downtime caused by defects
-      reinspection of work
c.   Appraisal costs
-      receiving inspection
-      setup for testing
-      quality audits
d.   Prevention costs
-      quality engineering
-      statistical process control
-      quality improvement programs

Recommended Cases

1.   Analog Devices: The Half Life System (HBS case 190-061 and teaching note 5-191-103) relates to improving quality and reducing cycle time.

2.   Texas Eastman (HBS case 9-190-039; teaching note 5-191-064) illustrates how financial measures can support a firm's total quality management program.

3.   Texas Instruments: Cost of Quality (A) and (B) (HBS cases 189-029 and 189-111 and teaching note 5-189-112) pertain to the concept of cost of quality and implementing quality systems.

Chapter 10

Capital Budgeting

CENTRAL FOCUS AND LEARNING OBJECTIVES

Chapter 10 presents discusses issues related to investment in capital assets including:

1.   The importance of long-term assets

2.   The nature of capital budgeting, investment and return, the time value of money, future value, effective and nominal rates of interest, present value, annuities, cost of capital, net present value, and return on investment

3.   The effect of taxes on investment decisions

4.   The role and nature of what-if and sensitivity analysis

5.   The ways in which strategic considerations affect capital budgeting

6.   The role of postimplementation audits in capital budgeting

Chapter Overview

In this chapter, investment decisions related to capital assets are discussed. The chapter begins with a discussion of the importance of long-term or capital assets, and why their acquisition is important from an investment and return standpoint.

One of the most central ideas related to making investment in long-term assets is the time value of money. Core concepts related to the time value of money such as future value, effective and nominal rates of interest, present value, present and future value of annuities, the cost of capital, net present value, how to evaluate an investment proposal, return on investment, and the effect of taxes are well-illustrated.

Strategic considerations such as producing a product or delivering a service that competitors cannot make, improving the quality of a product by reducing errors, and shortening the cycle time to make a product all should be considered when a long-term capital asset decision is being made. Other topics include the use of what-if and sensitivity analysis and the role of postimplementation audits for capital budgeting decisions.

Chapter Outline _____

> Central to understanding capital budgeting decisions, students must understand the time value of money. Many may already have studied time value concepts, but from my experience, a thorough review will solidify their understanding. Thus, I would spend quite a bit of time nailing down the most basic issues relating to present and future value. Note also that the readings for this section focus primarily on justifying new technology and thinking about technology's contribution to product costs.

Learning Objective 1: The importance of long-term assets. DO MULTIPLE CHOICE QUESTION 1.

I.   The Importance of Long-Term (Capital) Assets

The focus in this chapter is on investments in long-term assets. Long-term assets create the committed costs that we have labeled batch-related, product- and process-related and facility-sustaining.

    A.   **Long-term or capital assets** are equipment or facilities that provide productive services to the organization for more than one period.

II.   Why is the Acquisition of Long-Term Assets Important?

    A.   Organizations commit to long-term assets for long periods of time.

    B.   The amount of capital committed is usually very large.

    C.   The long-term nature of capital assets creates technological risk for organizations.

    D.   **Capital budgeting** is the collection of tools planners use to evaluate the acquisition of long-term assets based on the above considerations.

E.   The **payback period** is the number of years taken for the cash inflows associated with a project to recover the initial investment.

Learning Objective 2: The nature of capital budgeting, investment and return, the time value of money, future value, effective and nominal rates of interest, present value, annuities, cost of capital, net present value, and return on investment. DO MULTIPLE CHOICE QUESTIONS 2, 3, 4, 5 and 6.

Readings in Management Accounting

James Brimson's "Technology Accounting," (Reading 10.1) suggests that the costs of technology are traceable and should be included as prime product costs.

III.   Investment and Return

A.   **Investment** is the monetary value of the assets that the organization gives up to acquire a long-term asset.

B.   **Return** is the increased cash flows in the future as a result of the long-term asset acquired.

IV.   Time Value of Money

A.   The **time value of money** is the idea that, because money can be invested to earn a return, the value of money depends on when it is received.

B.   **Future value** is the amount to which a sum invested today will accumulate over a stated number of periods and at a stated rate of interest.

Future value of an investment in 1 year   =

Investment * (1 + Annual rate of interest)

C. **Compounding effect (of interest)** is the phenomenon of earning interest on interest that was previously earned over multiple periods.

Future value of an investment in n periods =

Investment $* (1 + r)^n$

where r is the rate of return

 Review Exhibit 10-1 and Equation 10.1 on the compounding process.

D. Effective and Nominal Rates of Interest.

1. The **nominal rate of interest** is the stated annual rate of interest.

2. The **effective rate of interest** is the actual annual rate of interest earned on an investment.

The effective rate of interest r_e is computed as follows:

$$r_e = (1 + \frac{r_n}{n})^n - 1$$

where r_n is the nominal interest rate and n is the number of compounding periods.

Readings in Management Accounting

Robert Kaplan's, "Must CIM Be Justified By Faith Alone?" (Reading 10.2) argues that justification for computer-integrated manufacturing can be done using discounted cash flow analysis and does not have to rely on beliefs or acts of faith. The article also can be used later when discussing strategic issues.

E. Present Value

1. **Present value** is the current monetary worth of an amount to be paid in the future under stated conditions of interest and compounding.

Present value =

Future amount received in period n

$$\overline{(1 + \text{Required periodic return})^n}$$

2. **Inflows** are the incremental cash inflows associated with an asset.

3. **Outflows** are the incremental cash outflows associated with an asset.

4. **Time zero (or period zero)** is the point of time when the investment is undertaken.

5. **Discounting** is the process of computing present value.

F. Present Value and Future Value of Annuities

1. An **annuity** is a contract that promises to pay a fixed amount each period for a stated number of periods.

2. **Discount rate** the interest rate used to compute present values.

3. The present value of an annuity is equal to:

Periodic annuity amount $\quad * \quad \dfrac{(1 + r)^n - 1}{r * (1 + r)^n}$

Make sure that you understand all of the formulae that have been presented. Work through the examples provided in the text.

G. Cost of Capital

1. The **cost of capital** is the minimum return that the organization must earn on its investments in order to meet its investors' return requirements.

H. Net Present Value and Evaluating An Investment Proposal

1. **Net present value** is the sum of the present values of all the cash inflows and cash outflows associated with a project (also called residual income, economic income, and economic value added).

2. **Period length** is the time period over which interest is computed (e.g. monthly, quarterly, semi-annually, or annual) in a capital budgeting analysis.

3. **Incremental cash flows** are cash flows that change as a result of acquiring, or disposing of, a long-term asset.

 Under net present value, six steps are used to determine the desirability of an investment proposal. These are (1) Choose the period length, (2) Identify the firm's cost of capital, (3) Identify the incremental cash flows for each period, (4) Compute the present value of each period's cash flows, (5) Sum the project's cash inflows and outflows and determine the net present value, and (6) If the net present value is positive, then the project is acceptable from an economic perspective.

I.   Return on Investment

        1.   **Return on investment** is the discount rate that makes a project's net present value equal zero (also known as the internal rate of return).

Learning Objective 3: The effect of taxes on investment decisions. DO MULTIPLE CHOICE QUESTION 7.

J.   The Effect of Taxes

        1.   The focus of the discussion in this section is on the effects of depreciation on taxes. Depreciation acts as a tax shield in that it offsets some of the taxes that would be paid.

$$\text{Depreciation} = \frac{\text{Initial Investment} - \text{Salvage Value}}{\text{Project Life}}$$

 Review the examples in Exhibit 10-5 on Wendy's Pizza Parlour and Exhibit 10-6 on Karl's Taxi.

Learning Objective 4: The role and nature of what-if and sensitivity analysis. DO MULTIPLE CHOICE QUESTION 8.

V.   What-If and Sensitivity Analysis

        1.   **What-if analysis** is the process of varying the assumptions underlying a forecasting model to determine the effects of those assumptions on the forecasted amounts.

        2.   **Sensitivity analysis** is the process of varying the assumptions underlying a decision to determine the decision's sensitivity to those assumptions.

Learning Objective 5: The ways in which strategic considerations affect capital budgeting. DO MULTIPLE CHOICE QUESTION 9.

Readings in Management Accounting

Reading 10.3, John Shank and Vijay Govindarajan's "Strategic Cost Analysis of Technological Investments" links strategic cost management with capital investment analysis.

VI. Strategic Considerations

The key benefits provided by a long-term asset are:

1.   producing a product or providing a service that competitors cannot.

2.   Improving the quality of a product by reducing the potential to make mistakes.

3.   Reducing the cycle time required to make a product.

Learning Objective 6: The role of postimplementation audits in capital budgeting. DO MULTIPLE CHOICE QUESTION 10.

VII. Postimplementation Audits and Capital Budgeting

1.   A **post-implementation audit** is an opportunity to reevaluate a past decision to purchase a long-lived asset by comparing expected and actual inflows and outflows. The audit provides the following benefits:

a.   By comparing estimates with results, planners can determine why their estimates were incorrect and avoid making the same mistakes in the future.

b.   Rewards can be given to those who make good capital budgeting decisions.

c.   If the audit is not done, there are no controls on planners who might be tempted to inflate the benefits to get their projects approved.

Chapter Quiz/Demonstration Exercises _____

1. Which of the following statements is false regarding long-term assets?

    (a) Long-term assets are committed for extendend periods of time.
    (b) Acquiring long-term assets creates significant financial risks for organizations.
    (c) Acquiring long-term capital assets creates technological risk for organizations.
    (d) Flexible budgeting is the collection of tools that planners use to evaluate the acquisition of long-term assets.

2. Although not as theoretically sound as other methods, the _____ method is the most commonly used method for making investment decisions.

    (a) return on investment
    (b) payback
    (c) net present value
    (d) sensitivity

3. What is the the future value of $1 nine years from now at an interest rate of 6%?

    (a) $1.69
    (b) $1.65
    (c) $1.50
    (d) $1.06

4. As of December 31, 1995, Pasadena Credit Company promises a nominal annual rate of return of 17%. On January 1, 1996 the Pasadena Credit Company promises a nominal rate of interest of 17% and decides to pay interest quarterly. What is the effective annual rate of interest?

    (a) 17%
    (b) 16.73%
    (c) 18.39%
    (d) 20.06%

5. Anita and Neil want to accumulate $70,000 for their newborn child's education over the next 16 years. How much money at a 7% interest rate do they have to invest now to accumulate the $70,000.

   (a) $21,654.89
   (b) $4,375
   (c) $10,987.11
   (d) $23,711.42

6. The definition of the cost of capital is:

   (a) the sum of the present values of all cash inflows and outflows associated with a project.
   (b) the maximum return an organization must earn on it investments in order to meet its investor's return requirements.
   (c) the minimum return an organization must earn on its investments in order to meet its investor's return requirements.
   (d) the same as that for the return on investment.

7. The Sydney Lumber Company has a before-tax cash flow of $900,000 in 1995. It also has depreciation expense of $235,000 and its income is taxed at the rate of 38%. What is the after-tax cash flow for 1995?

   (a) $647,300
   (b) $483,200.
   (c) $282,750.
   (d) $323,700.

8. An analysis that determines the effect of a change in a parameter on a result is called:

   (a) present value analysis.
   (b) what-if analysis.
   (c) capital investment analysis.
   (d) future value analysis.

9. Which of the following is not one of the more common strategic benefits provided by acquiring long-term assets?

    (a) Being able to deliver a product or service that competitors cannot.

    (b) Improving product quality.

    (c) Reducing the number of short-run decisions made about operations.

    (d) Reducing cycle time.

10. Postimplementation audits of capital budgeting decisions have the following benefits, EXCEPT:

    (a) Planners will be encouraged to take on more risky investments.

    (b) Managers can identify and reward those who are good at making these types of decisions.

    (c) Planners can identify where their estimates were incorrect.

    (d) Planners will be more reluctant to inflate their estimates of benefits.

Solutions to Chapter Quiz/Demonstration Exercises _____

1. d.
2. b.
3. a.
4. c.
5. d.
6. c.
7. a.
8. b.
9. c.
10. a.

SYNOPSIS OF *READINGS IN MANAGEMENT ACCOUNTING* AND QUESTIONS TO ASSIGN WITH SUGGESTED ANSWERS

Synopsis of Readings in Management Accounting

In his article, "*Must CIM Be Justified by Faith Alone*" (Reading 10.1), Robert Kaplan states that a growing number of managers have been unsuccessful in applying traditional types of financial analysis such as discounted cash flow (DCF) analysis to investments such as computer-integrated manufacturing (CIM). The lack of success has caused many to believe that their intuition and their faith in new technology will guide them in CIM-related decisions. Kaplan argues that, in many instances, DCF has been inappropriately applied because managers have set arbitrarily high hurdle rates for new investments, compared the investment in CIM to doing nothing at all, and focused more on incremental improvements in new technology rather than on revolutionary change. According to Kaplan, the decision to invest in CIM can be quantified and other non-traditional variables such as improved quality, greater flexibility, reduced inventory and floor space, and lower throughput times should all be factored into the decision. The real challenge that Kaplan sees is that managers have to improve their abilities to estimate and evaluate the costs and benefits of CIM and not discard DCF because of lack of knowledge or understanding.

In a related vein, James Brimson's article on "*Technology Accounting*" (Reading 10.2), considers a new approach to accounting for new technology. According to Brimson, the current state of technology accounting relates solely to capital asset depreciation. This may have been appropriate when technology costs were minor compared to direct labor costs, but today, technology costs are a much larger percentage of product costs and much more accurate methods are needed to account for them. Brimson rejects traditional time-based depreciation methods such as straight-line depreciation and suggests that the choice of methods should be based on the relationship between assets and the manufacturing process. Finally, Brimson argues that, given a higher degree of traceability, technology should be treated as a direct cost similar to direct labor and direct materials.

Synopsis of Readings in Management Accounting

Reading 10.3, John Shank and Vijay Govindarajan's "*Strategic Cost Analysis of Technological Investment*," builds on both of the previous papers and suggests a strategic cost management approach to investing in new technology. Arguing that all previous approaches are lacking in one way or another, Shank and Govindarajan incorporate the ideas of value chain, cost driver, and competitive advantage into an expanded financial analysis framework. Combining these three types of ideas and analyses overcomes a central limitation of other proposed frameworks, i.e. which is the failure to incorporate a firm's strategy clearly into technological investment decisions. The article provides several illustrations of how the framework can be successfully applied.

Points to Include in Answering Questions from the Readings

1. What are the intangible benefits of CIM that Kaplan says often are ignored in traditional investment analysis?

    Student answers should include:
    a. greater flexibility - benefits of economies of scope or the potential for low cost production of high-variety, low volume goods.
    b. shorter throughput and lead time - CIM reduces these variables.
    c. increased learning - experience can be gained by managers working with and understanding new technologies.

    Overall, while difficult to quantify, these intangible benefits have a greater than zero value, especially when trying to assess the benefits leads to a broadening of managerial experience and understanding.

2. Brimson says that time-based depreciation is popular for two reasons. What are the reasons and are there better alternatives?

    Student answers should include:
    a. Time-based methods guarantee that the cost of technology will be recovered at the end of its depreciable life.
    b. People tend to equate time with cost and time-based methods are consistent with this view.

    There are better alternatives related to increasing the accuracy between technological and product costs. Time-based methods have a distant relationship to product costs. Since technological costs are increasing and direct labor costs are decreasing a much clearer assignment of technological costs is warranted.

Points to Include in Answering Questions from the Readings

3. What are the four approaches to evaluating technological investments that Shank and Govindarajan critique? What are the problems with each approach?

    Student answers should include:
    a. Discard all formal financial analysis - this is very ad hoc and there are techniques available that will provide better results.
    b. Use a refined NPV model - but not enough strategic variables are included in this approach.
    c. Michael Porter's framework - links technological decisions to strategy, but explicit attention to financial analysis is not given.
    d. Bromwich and Bhimani integrated strategic-financial framework - Shank and Govindarajan argue that this approach, while going in the right direction is not detailed enough regarding the evaluation of technological investments.

Recommended Cases

1. I recommend a series of cases on capital budgeting from Rotch, Allen and Smith's casebook including:

      a.   Lake Erie Corporation (basic case on cash flow analysis)
      b.   East Tacoma Works (a decision to purchase a new crane)
      c.   Prillman Lumber Company (more advanced case)
      d.   Southern Railway: Verta-Pak (advanced case).

2. Del Norte Paper Co. (C) (HBS cases 9-177-036). A comprehensive description of an on-going capital budgeting system and problems that it faces from foreign subsidiaries.

3 Burlington Northern: The ARES Decision (A) and (B) (HBS cases 9-191-122 (A) ; teaching note 5-193-034 and 9-191-123 (B); teaching note 5-193-034). This is an advanced case set in the railroad industry.

Chapter 11

Planning and Control

CENTRAL FOCUS AND LEARNING OBJECTIVES

Chapter 11 presents an overview of planning and control issues including:

1. The concept of an organization as an open system that must adapt to its environment to be successful and survive.

2. The nature and interrelationship of organization planning and control.

3. The ways that organizations develop goals to reflect the requirements of the stakeholders whom the organization is committed to serving.

4. The different types and classifications of control systems.

5. The critical role of performance measurement in control.

6. The importance of self-regulating systems and employee involvement in control.

Chapter Overview

In chapter 11 a wide variety of issues and problems are discussed in relation to the topics of planning and control. Planning provides the road map for where an organization is going, while control consists of a series of tools that guide the way and provide progress reports about the trip.

One central idea that is discussed is the balanced scorecard. This is a set of performance targets and results that reflect the organization's performance in meeting its objectives. The term "balanced" refers to consideration of both the owner's and customer's perspectives and the use of quantitative and qualitative measures.

A number of other topics are presented including the role of an organization's mission statement, various forms of control including task and results control, how controls vary as a result of the level in the organization that one is managing, and self-control.

Finally, the role of management accounting is supporting employee involvement systems, management by objectives and total quality management are described. These topics will be discussed further in Chapter 14 on behavioral and organizational issues.

Chapter Outline _____

> The topics of planning and control are central to management accounting and have become even more integrated as activity-based costing and management and other performance measures such as quality and flexibility come under the management accounting umbrella.

> **Learning Objective 1:** The concept of an organization as an open system that must adapt to its environment to be successful and survive. DO MULTIPLE CHOICE QUESTION 1.

I. Organizations as Adaptive Systems

In today's business environment, organizations must view themselves as open systems and take advantage of opportunities and monitor threats.

    A.   An **opportunity** is a change in the organization's environment that enhances its ability to achieve its goals. A change in customer tastes is an opportunity.

    B.   A **threat** is a change in the organization's environment that diminishes its ability to achieve its goals. A new competitor is a threat.

> **Learning Objective 2:** The nature and interrelationship of organization planning and control. DO MULTIPLE CHOICE QUESTIONS 2 and 3.

II. The Need for Planning and Control

Both planning and control are key concepts in management accounting.

    A.   **Planning** is the way in which organizations set their goals and objectives, and helps identify where an organization is going.

B.   **Controls** are the methods by which organizations keep themselves on track regarding their goals and objectives.

III.   Strategic Planning

A.   **Strategic planning** is the tools and processes an organization uses to identify its goals.

1.   **Goals** are the long-term results sought by an organization.

2.   **Strength** is a characteristic or resource that offers the organization an advantage successfully pursuing its goals. Highly motivated employees are a strength.

3.   **Weakness** is an organization characteristic or liability that inhibits the organization from pursuing its goals. A bad public image is a weakness.

B.   A **corporate-level strategy** is developed by upper level management, and is a broad statement of the type of product or service markets where the organization has chosen to compete. For example, a decision to compete only in the domestic automobile market is a corporate-level strategy for an automobile manufacturer.

C.   A **business-level strategy** is developed by middle level management, and is a statement of how the organization has chosen to compete in its chosen markets. A decision to be the low cost producer and price leader is a business level strategy.

D.   A **functional-level strategy** is a statement of how the organization carries out its business level strategy daily at the operational level. Using just-in-time manufacturing is an example of a functional level strategy.

Readings in Management Accounting

Robert S. Kaplan and David P. Norton's "The Balanced Scorecard - Measures that Drive Performance," (Reading 11.1) presents the original article from which much of the text material was derived.

IV.   The Balanced Scorecard

   A.   **The balanced scorecard** is a set of performance targets and an approach to performance measurement that stresses meeting all the organization's objectives relating to its critical success factors. Balanced refers to the incorporation of both firm owner's and their customer's perspectives.

   B.   Different Stakeholder Roles

          There are two general roles for stakeholders:

          1.   Those that play an active role in shaping the organization's success, such as employees and suppliers.

          2.   Those who define the environment in which the organization operates such as customers, shareholders and the community.

Ask students how the concept of the balanced scorecard be applied to (a) a hospital emergency room, (b) a restaurant and (c) a physician's office? Have them think of a variety of performance measures for each setting.

   C.   The Preeminence of the Customer

          Of all stakeholder groups, the most important is the customer. The organization's ability to meets all of its stakeholder's needs is decided by its success in satisfying its customers.

D.   Conflicting Stakeholder Goals

Senior management must be able to take responsibility to identify and resolve any conflicts that may arise between diverse groups of stakeholders.

Readings in Management Accounting

John Pearce and Fred David's "Corporate Mission Statements: The Bottom Line," (Reading 11.2) explores the linkage between having a mission statement and organizational performance.

Learning Objective 3: The ways that organizations develop goals to reflect the requirements of the stakeholders whom the organization is committed to serving. DO MULTIPLE CHOICE QUESTION 4.

V.   The Organization's Mission Statement

A.   A **mission statement** is the organization's statement of purpose and commitment to its stakeholders. The statement identifies:

1.   Who matters to the organization.

2.   The **critical success factors** of the organization. **Critical success factors** are the facets of an organization's performance critical in meeting the commitments that the organization has made to its stakeholders. Critical success factors include cost, quality, and service for most organizations.

VI.   From Planning to Control

   A.   **Control** is the set of tools and processes an organization uses to assess and improve its progress toward achieving its goals.

      1.   The **focus of control** is on the organization's goals or process objectives identified during planning.

      2.   The **object of control** is the set of performance measures that allow the organization to monitor its progress towards meeting its objectives.

      3.   Planning and control systems have five common steps:

         a.   Setting *goals*.

         b.   *Measuring* performance.

         c.   *Comparing* performance to goals and computing the differences (or variances) between them.

         d.   *Analyzing* the variances.

         e.   Taking action and *correcting* the causes of the variances.

 Review Exhibit 11-2 for an illustration of how planning and control are related.

Learning Objective 4: The different types and classifications of control systems DO MULTIPLE CHOICE QUESTION 5

VII.   The Cycle, or Timing, of Control

   Controls can be classified by their timing relative to the controlled event.

A. **Feedforward control** is often called preventive control, this approach to control focuses on preventing an undesired outcome and occurs before the activity is undertaken.

B. **Concurrent control** is an approach to control that relies on detecting problems when they are happening so that the process can be adjusted to prevent further undesired outcomes.

C. **Feedback control** is an approach to control that reports data on completed activities to decide whether they were completed as planned.

Readings in Management Accounting

Ken Merchant's "The Control Function of Management," (Reading 11.3) illustrates a framework for control tools including action, results and personnel controls.

Learning Objective 5: The critical role of performance measurement in control. DO MULTIPLE CHOICE QUESTIONS 6, 7 and 8.

VIII. Control Methods

To achieve goals an organizational unit can be told what to do (task control) or it can be asked to use its resources and knowledge to achieve its goals (results control):

A. **Task control** consists of systems or procedures designed to ensure that employees follow stated procedures or rules.

1. The **environment** consists of the elements of the system outside the organization that affects the organization's ability to achieve its goals.

2.   Internal control procedures are systems and rules used to enforce or promote task control.

B.   **Results control** is a system focused on results or outcomes that is designed to motivate decision making to achieve the organization's goals.

1.   The advantages of a results control system are:

a.   Employees' knowledge and skills are used to the organization's advantage in meeting its goals.

b.   It involves employees in decision-making which may make them much more supportive of the organization's goals.

2.   The disadvantages of a results control system are:

a.   A **controllability** problem may arise. This means that uncontrollable factors may occur in the employee's environment which can make performance measurement very difficult.

b.   In group settings with group goals a **free rider** problem may develop. This occurs when some employees will benefit and others will suffer depending on the dynamics within the group. For example, some employees will work hard and others will not, but if the goal is achieved the employees who did not work obtain the same reward as those who did.

c.   An **externality** problem can arise when the performance of one group can affect the results reported by another.

C.   **Critical performance indicators** are the measures an organization uses to monitor and assess its performance on its critical success factors. To be most beneficial to employees, critical performance indicators must:

1.   be comprehensive in measuring all facets of the job.

2. reflect how each job contributes to the organization's success.

3. reflect how the employee thinks about his or her job.

 Review Exhibit 11-3 for a summary of the differences between task and results control.

D. Results Control at the Various Levels of the Organization.

1. Results control at the **lower level** of the organization.

    Control and performance are focused on managing daily activities that create the organization's products including the process elements related to meeting customer requirements. Variables such as quality and response time are assessed.

2. Results control at the **middle management level** of the organization.

    At this level control and performance are related to how well the organization is meeting its commitments to different stakeholder groups and how well the operating systems are functioning to meet these needs. Variables such as meeting customer delivery requirements, cycle time performance, are cost performance monitored.

3. Results control at the **upper level** of the organization.

    Control and performance are tied directly to meeting long-term performance and aggregate results. More global questions related to the direction of the organization, whether it is meeting its social as well as financial responsibilities are determined.

Exhibit 11-4 illustrates the linkages between organizational level, type of responsibility and the type of performance measure, while 11-5 focuses on the correspondence between critical success factors and critical performance indicators at the organization's upper level.

Learning Objective 6: The importance of self-regulating systems and employee involvement in control. DO MULTIPLE CHOICE QUESTIONS 9 and 10.

IX.   Self-Control.

A.   **Self-Control** is the ability of a system to accept objectives and regulate itself as it seeks to achieve those objectives. For this type of system to work, three things must be in place:

1.   The formal planning system must have identified the organization's critical success factors and disseminated them to all employees.

2.   The organization must have an excellent performance measurement system that measures performance on each unit's critical success factors.

3.   The organization must hire well-trained and highly motivated people who are empowered to suggest changes and make improvements.

X.   The Role of Management Accounting in Supporting Employee Involvement Systems

Management accountants must:

A.   Make sure that the organization's control system conveys its critical success factors to all organizational members.

B.   Ensure that the linkages between the organization's critical performance indictors to its critical success factors are secure and meaningful.

C.   Assess the critical performance indicators and ensure that they are measured consistently and accurately.

XI.   Management By Objectives (MBO)

A.   **Management by objectives** is a control system that uses the idea of self-control in an environment of employee involvement to promote results control.

 While MBO differs depending on each firm, go over the seven steps in the text as an example of a typical procedure.

 Readings in Management Accounting

"Revolution in Management Control," by Gerald Ross (Reading 11.4) discusses a number of new issues facing management control systems design

XII.   Integrated Control Systems

A.   **Total quality management** also known as total quality control and TQM, this is a results control system that is widely used, in various forms, to focus an organization on meeting customer requirements.

The elements of total quality management include:

1.   Focus on the customer's needs and wants.

2.   Measure your own performance from the customer's point of view.

3. Document all activities and increase their efficiency and effectiveness.

4. Involve everyone in the organization to make improvements and to increase commitment.

5. Establish specific goals and objectives to promote an understanding of the organization's goals.

Chapter Quiz/Demonstration Exercises _____

1. The following statements are true about open systems, EXCEPT:

    (a) Open systems are better able to adapt to their environments.
    (b) Open systems are able to deal with both threats and opportunities in the environment.
    (c) Open systems interact with their environments.
    (d) Open systems are more self-contained than closed systems.

2. Of the following which is not a part of the overall strategic planning process.

    (a) business-level strategy.
    (b) functional level strategy.
    (c) enterprise-level strategy.
    (d) corporate-level strategy.

3. The term "balanced" in the balanced scorecard approach reflects:

    (a) both owner and employee perspectives.
    (b) both owner and customer perspectives.
    (c) both owner and shareholder perspectives
    (d) both business partner and owner perspectives.

4. Mission statements identify each of the following, EXCEPT:

    (a) the organization's strategic plan.
    (b) the organization's guiding principles, beliefs and values.
    (c) the organization's critical success factors.
    (d) the organization's stakeholders.

5. Which of the following is the strongest form of control?

    (a) Concurrent control.
    (b) Feedforward control.
    (c) Feedback control.
    (d) Internal control.

6. A process or method designed to enforce compliance with stated organization rules _____ control.

    (a) results
    (b) personnel
    (c) task
    (d) self

7. Each of the following are characteristics of critical performance indicators, EXCEPT:

    (a) They must reflect how a job contributes to the organization's success.
    (b) They must reflect how the job's incumbent thinks about the job.
    (c) They must focus only on qualitative measures of performance.
    (d) They are comprehensive in measuring all facets of a job.

8. Which of the following pairs of critical success factors and critical performance indicators are the most poorly matched?

	Critical success factor	Critical performance indicator
(a)	cost	cost as a percentage of sales revenue
(b)	quality	customer satisfaction ratings
(c)	service	number of on-time deliveries
(d)	cost	number of returned items

9. Each of the following factors for critical for self-control to be successful, EXCEPT:

    (a) The organization must have an excellent performance measurement system that measures performance on the critical success factors.
    (b) The organization must use results and not task control.
    (c) The organization must employ well-trained and motivated employees who will help the organization improve.
    (d) The formal planning system must have identified the organization's critical success factors.

10. Management by objectives involves each of the following, EXCEPT:

(a) Superiors instruct each responsibility unit in its contribution to the organization.

(b) Precise and measurable critical performance indicators assess the role or contribution of each responsibility unit.

(c) Superiors ask each responsibility unit to identify how it contributes to the organization's goals.

(d) Each responsibility unit develops, with its superior, specific performance objectives on each of its critical performance indicators.

Solutions to Chapter Quiz/Demonstration Exercises _____

1. d.
2. c.
3. b.
4. a.
5. b.
6. c.
7. c.
8. d.
9. b.
10. a.

SYNOPSIS OF *READINGS IN MANAGEMENT ACCOUNTING* AND QUESTIONS TO ASSIGN WITH SUGGESTED ANSWERS

Synopsis of Readings in Management Accounting

Robert Kaplan and David Norton's article, "*The Balanced Scorecard - Measures that Drive Performance*" (Reading 11.1) begins this chapter's readings. The authors state that the scorecard concept addresses four questions: (1) How do customers see us? (customer perspective), (2) What must we excel at? (internal perspective), (3) Can we continue to improve and create value? (innovation and learning perspective), and (4) How do we look to shareholders? (financial perspective). For each of these perspectives, organizations can develop their own goals and measures. Kaplan and Norton liken the scorecard to the dials and indicators in a plane's cockpit. By having a comprehensive set of measures together in one place, management can more readily see what is occurring simultaneously in various critical areas of their organizations.

Reading 11.2 by John Pearce and Fred David, entitled "*Corporate Mission Statements: The Bottom Line*," presents the results of an empirical study of corporate mission statements. Using data gathered from the mission statements of 61 Fortune 500 firms, the article compares the actual content of mission statements to eight components that the authors state should be included in mission statements. Results show that many of the eight components were included, the one surprise being that only 20% of the mission statements mentioned what their core technologies were. Pearce and David also performed an analysis of the relationship between the frequency of components mentioned and firm financial performance. Their major finding was that significantly more of the mission statements of the highest performing firms exhibited three of the eight components than the statements of the lowest performing firms. The authors view their work as preliminary and suggest that much more research needs to be conducted before clear conclusions can be drawn.

Synopsis of Readings in Management Accounting

Kenneth Merchant's "*The Control Function of Management*" (Reading 11.3) presents a framework for determining the appropriate use of management controls. Merchant discusses specific action controls, those designed to make sure that individuals take the most appropriate actions; controls over results, those related to meeting targets such as budgets; and personnel controls, those based on hiring people who will do what is best for the organization. Using this framework, Merchant discusses a number of topics including how to choose among the various forms of control, and the kinds of financial and behavioral costs are incurred in using each form of control.

Gerald Ross writes, in "*Revolution in Management Control*" (Reading 11.4), that management control systems are in a state of revolution due to two major factors: changes in technology and changes in the marketplace. The technological changes that Ross refers to relate to the shift from standardized repetitive manufacturing to much more flexible operations, while marketplace changes pertain to the shift from mass market to mass customization. These changes also signal a need for the redesign of management accounting and control systems. New designs should incorporate real time controls rather than after the fact controls and peer pressure and social controls should supplant traditional top down control.

Points to Include in Answering Questions from the Readings

1. According to Kaplan and Norton, what are the four perspectives on which the balanced scorecard is built, and how do they differ?

   Student answers should include:
   a. Financial Perspective - How do we look to shareholders?
   b. Internal Business Perspective - What must we excel at?
   c. Customer Perspective - How do our customers see us?
   d. Innovation and Learning Perspective - Can we continue to improve and create value?

2. List the eight components of corporate mission statements. Of the eight which three were most commonly mentioned in mission statements studied the Pearce and David?

   Student answers should include:
   a. Target customers and markets.
   b. Principal products or services.
   c. Geographic Domain.
   d. Core technologies.
   e. Concern for survival, growth and profitability.
   f. Company philosophy.
   g. Company self-concept.
   h. Desired public image.

   The most commonly mentioned components were (a) Target customers and markets, (f) company philosophy and (g) company self-concept.

Points to Include in Answering Questions from the Readings

3.   Merchant discusses specific action, results, and personnel controls. Provide three examples of each.

Student answers should include:
a.   specific action controls consist of:
- behavioral constraints (locks)
- action accountability (work rules)
- procedures (codes of conduct)
b.   results controls consist of:
- results accountability (standards of performance)
- results accountability (budget attainment)
- management by objectives (MBO)
c.   personnel controls consist of:
- upgrading capabilities (selection, training)
- improve communications (clarify expectations)
- encourage peer control (shared goals)

4   Ross suggests that, to be relevant in the 1990s, management accounting must be based on a different set of principles about human behavior. What are these?

Student answers should include:
a.   Put control where the operation is.
b.   Use real time rather than after-the-fact controls
c.   Rebuild the assumptions underlying management accounting to build trust rather than distrust.
d.   Move to control based on peer norms.
e.   Rebuild the incentive systems to reinforce responsiveness and teamwork.

Recommended Cases

1. I suggest the following cases from Rotch, Allen and Smith's casebook: Gamma Company (introductory management control case), B-3-3 (control system design in the public sector), Pepsico International (an overview management control case).

2 One of my favorites is Ken Merchant's Controls at the Sands Hotel and Casino (HBS case 9-184-048 and teaching note 5-188-069). Ken Merchant has also developed a number of cases at the University of Southern California. To obtain a listing write to Professor Ken Merchant, Dean, School of Accounting, University of Southern California 90089-1421.

3. Chadwick, Inc.: The Balanced Scorecard (HBS case 9-193-091) is a good illustration of the concept. Another reference is by Robert Kaplan and David Norton, "Putting the Balanced Scorecard to Work," Harvard Business Review (September-October 1993), pp. 134-147.

Chapter 12

Financial Control

CENTRAL FOCUS AND LEARNING OBJECTIVES

This chapter discusses numerous aspects of financial control including:

1. The motives and issues underlying the design and use of responsibility centers in an organization.

2. The issues and basic tools used in assessing the performance of a responsibility center

3. The common forms of responsibility centers

4. The issues and problems created by revenue and cost interactions in evaluating the performance of an organization unit.

5. Transfer pricing

6. The use of return on investment and residual income as financial control tools

7. The limitations of using financial controls

Chapter Overview

As decision making becomes more decentralized, organizations have to devise ways to motivate managers and reduce as many across- division inconsistencies as possible. In chapter 12, we discuss the four major types of responsibility centers, cost centers and the use of flexible budgets, revenue centers, profit centers and investment centers.

The concept of controllability is introduced along with segment margin reporting and transfer pricing. A number of forms of transfer pricing exist including market-based transfers, cost-based transfers, negotiated transfer prices, and administered transfer prices.

The return on investment concept introduced in Chapter 1 is presented in much more depth and two alternatives, the residual income approach and shareholder value analysis (or economic value analysis) are illustrated.

Chapter Outline _____

> Evaluating managerial performance in different kinds of responsibility centers has to be done carefully. Apprise students that the notion of responsibility and controllability are critical to this chapter.

I.   The Role and Contribution of Financial Control

This chapter discusses issues relating to using financial information in the process of organizational control.

Learning Objective 1: The motives and issues underlying the design and use of responsibility centers in an organization. DO MULTIPLE CHOICE QUESTION 1.

II. Decentralization

A.   **Centralization** occurs when decision-making is reserved for senior managers. Typically centralization works effectively in organizations who face stable environments and technologies and where customer requirements were well-understood.

B.   **Decentralization** is the strategy of delegating decision making responsibility from senior management to employees at lower levels of the organization. Decentralization is effective in organizations whose environments, technologies and customer requirements are constantly changing.

III. Operations and Financial Control

A.   **Operations control** views control from the point of view of process improvements.

B.   **Financial control** is the formal evaluation of some financial facet of an organization or a responsibility center. Financial control helps identify the poor performing areas of an organization and suggests where improvements can be made.

Learning Objective 2: The issues and basic tools used in assessing the performance of a responsibility center. DO MULTIPLE CHOICE QUESTION 2.

IV.   The Role of Responsibility Centers

A **responsibility center** is an organizational subunit for which a manager has been assigned accountability in the form of cost (a cost center), revenue (a revenue center), profits (a profit center), or return on investment (an investment center).

Learning Objective 3: The common forms of responsibility centers. DO MULTIPLE CHOICE QUESTIONS 3, 4 and 5.

A.   Cost Centers

A **cost center** is a responsibility center whose employees control costs but do not control its revenues or investment level.

1.   Comparing Budgeted and Actual Results

When budgeted and actual results are compared variances can arise. When actual costs are greater than budgeted costs an unfavorable variance occurs (see chapter 6), but when the budgeted costs are greater than actual costs, a favorable variance exists.

Review Exhibits 12-1, 12-2 and 12-3 for simple variance analyses. Note in particular that when actual and planned production volume differs, variance analysis is inappropriate. The flexible budget concept can overcome this problem.

Readings in Management Accounting

Y. T. Mak and Melvin Roush, "Flexible Budgeting and Variance Analysis in an Activity-Based Costing Environment," (Reading 12.1) presents a good discussion of how ABC can be integrated with flexible budgeting.

Readings in Management Accounting

Robert Kaplan's "Flexible Budgeting in an Activity-Based Costing Framework," (Reading 12.2) also addresses the ABC and flexible budgeting issue extending previous work (see Reading 3.1).

2.   The Flexible Budget

The key concept in flexible budgeting is that cost targets in the planned or master budget is recast to reflect the actual level of production.   This allows comparisons of costs by holding volume constant. Without holding volume constant, a manager is comparing "apples to oranges," (costs at differing volume levels), rather than "apples to apples," (costs at the same volume levels).

    Review Exhibits 12-4 and 12-5 to understand the "apples to apples" comparison.

B. Revenue Centers

A **revenue center** is a responsibility center whose employees control revenues but do not control costs or the level of investment. Revenue centers can control the mix of items carried in their stores, prices of products and promotional activities. Revenue center managers are often at the mercy of others who determine the costs of their goods (e.g. a service station manager has no control over the cost of the gas it sells).

C. Profit Centers

A **profit center** is a responsibility center whose employees control revenues and costs but not the level of investment. The level of investment is usually controlled by senior management. Many franchises are profit centers.

D. Investment Centers

An **investment center** is a responsibility center whose employees control its revenues, costs, and the level of investment. The investment center is essentially an independent business.

 Exhibit 12-6 summarizes the differences among the various types of responsibility centers.

Learning Objective 4. The issues and problems created by revenue and cost interactions in evaluating the performance of an organization unit. DO MULTIPLE CHOICE QUESTION 6.

V. Evaluating Responsibility Centers

A. **Controllability** is a principle often used in control, which asserts that people should only be held accountable for results that they can control. The main application of this principle is that a managers should not be held accountable for costs outside their control. One major difficulty in applying this occurs when revenues and costs are jointly earned or incurred. Separating these component revenues and costs can involve fairly intricate accounting procedures.

B. A **segment margin** is the level of controllable profit reported by an organizational unit or product line. Each unit's segment margin is an estimate of its short-term effect on the organization's profit.

Interpreting segment margins should be done carefully as:

1. Segment margins can represent highly aggregated summaries of each organizational unit's performance. Thus, other critical success factors should be used as well to assess performance.

2. Some segment reports contain fairly arbitrary numbers. Accountants call these **soft numbers** as they rest on subjective assumptions over which there can be legitimate disagreement.

3. The revenue figures often reflect assumptions and allocations that can be misleading. These assumptions relate to how the revenues that the organization earned are divided among the responsibility centers.

 Review Exhibit 12-7 on segment reporting at Earl's Motors. Note the breakdown of costs to arrive at the segment margin.

Learning Objective 5: Transfer pricing. DO MULTIPLE CHOICE QUESTIONS 7 and 8.

VI. Transfer Pricing

A. **Transfer pricing** is a set of tools and methods used to attribute revenues earned by the organization to organization sub-units. Common transfer pricing forms are cost, market, negotiated, and administered. *Transfer* *pricing can be very arbitrary, especially if there is a high degree of interaction among the various responsibility centers.*

There are four broad approaches to transfer pricing:

1.   Market-Based Transfer Prices

       Market prices provide an independent valuation of products that are transferred between divisions and reflects jointly earned revenue in a manner which reflects the markets assessment. One difficulty is that clear market prices often do not exist for many products.

2.   Cost-Based Transfer Prices

       If goods or services do not have clear market prices, transfer prices can be based on cost. Common methods include variable cost plus a markup, full cost, and full cost plus a markup.

       Some concerns about cost-based transfer prices are:

       a.   Economists argue that only marginal cost transfer prices are optimal and that any other method results in economic losses for the overall organization.

       b.   Cost-based transfer also does not focus on the intent of the transfer pricing system which is to allow computation of unit incomes.

       c.   Another issue is that cost-based transfers do not provide the appropriate economic guidance when operations are capacity constrained.

3.   Negotiated Transfer Prices

       When market prices do not exist another possibility is to allow divisions to negotiate transfer prices. Critics argue that these types of prices reflect both negotiating skills and economic considerations and not just economics alone.

In an economic sense, the optimal transfer price occurs when the purchasing division offers to pay the supplying division the **net realizable value** of the last unit supplied for all of the units supplied. The net realizable value is the difference between a product's revenue and the additional costs needed to put the product in the customer's hands. See Appendix 12-1 for a mathematical treatment of the optimal quantity to transfer.

4.   Administered Transfer Prices

Administered transfer prices are set by an arbitrator or by a rule or policy. Some find them appealing because they are easy to administer. An example is to use the variable cost of a product plus 25%. Other view these types of prices as unappealing because they are quite arbitrary.

 Review Exhibit 12-10 for a summary of transfer pricing approaches.

B.   Assigning and Valuing Assets in Investment Centers

Other problems associated with evaluating investment centers relate to how to assign responsibility for jointly used assets such as cash and plant and equipment and for jointly created assets such as accounts receivable. Once these assets are assigned a method of costing such as historical cost or replacement cost has to be used.

C.   Cost Allocations to Support Financial Control

Even with all of the problems with evaluating responsibility center income statements, many organizations do produce the statements. Each must be studied carefully and with a critical eye. One of the key issues involves allocating jointly incurred costs. Finding the most appropriate cost driver requires careful analysis as we have been stressing throughout the text.

 Review Exhibits 12-11 and 12-12 on Shirley's Grill to see how indirect costs are allocated based on different allocation bases.

Learning Objective 6: The use of return on investment and residual income as financial control tools. DO MULTIPLE CHOICE QUESTIONS 9 and 10.

D. Efficiency and Productivity Elements of Return on Investment

In chapter 1, we discussed Dupont's development of the return on investment (ROI) concept. The ROI concept is:

$$\text{ROI} = \text{Operating Income/Investment}$$

$$= \frac{\text{Operating Income}}{\text{Sales}} * \frac{\text{Sales}}{\text{Investment}}$$

$$= \text{Return on sales} * \text{Asset turnover}$$

$$= \text{Efficiency} * \text{Productivity}$$

1. **Efficiency** is a measure of an organization's ability to control costs. As shown above, in financial control, this is the ratio of earnings to sales.

2. **Productivity** is a ratio of output to input. In financial control, as shown above, this is the ratio of sales to investment.

 Exhibit 12-13 details the Dupont ROI Control System

E. Assessing Return on Investment

1. Using ratio trends

   a. Define what is meant by investment. A possibility is total assets minus accumulated depreciation.

   b. Compare an organization's ROI to its competitors.

   c. Decompose ROI into its efficiency and productivity measures and compare these to those of other organizations.

   d. This type of analysis can be very useful, but it is only a first step. *Ratio analysis does not identify a problem or a solution, rather it points to where analysis can begin.*

   e. ROI should be viewed as a method to evaluate the desirability of long-term investments, rather than as a way to measure short-term performance of a manager. Organizations have to design ROI measures so that a manager's goals do not conflict with those of the organization's in general. A situation to be avoided occurs when a manager could earn a good return on
   project, but turns the investment down because the return is not high enough for the organization.

 Review Exhibits 12-14 through 12-18 on Dorchester Manufacturing for an analysis of the use of ratio trends.

---

2. Using Residual Income

   Critics of ROI have suggested the concept of **residual income** as another approach to evaluating investments.

Residual income =

Accounting income - Cost of capital

An advantage of residual income is that managers are motivated not to turn down projects that are less than their targeted ROI. Instead they will undertake projects that will maximize residual income.

3.   Using Shareholder Value Analysis

Shareholder value analysis also known as economic value analysis, evaluates a product line's financial desirability using its residual income. This method computes the residual income for every major product line and evaluates its long-term financial desirability by using its residual income.

Learning Objective 7: The limitations of using financial controls.

Readings in Management Accounting

Mark Beischel and Richard Smith's "Linking the Shop Floor to the Top Floor," (Reading 12.3) illustrates well the concept of tying performance measures together throughout the organization.

VII.   The Efficacy of Financial Control

Financial control has been criticized for three reasons:

A.   Measures of financial control are too narrow and do not measure other important performance variables such as product or service quality, customer service, etc.

B.   Financial measures of control focus on the overall level of performance achieved on critical success factors, rather than on specific individual success factors. Thus, it is hard to decide how to improve on those measures.

C.   Many times financial control is too focused on short-term results. This is not a problem inherent to financial control, rather it is a problem relating to how financial control can be misused. A short-term focus can be debilitating for all employees, especially this kind of an orientation, produces behaviors that are not in the best long-run interests of the organization.

Chapter Quiz/Demonstration Exercises _____

1. Each of the following is true about decentralization, EXCEPT:

   (a) Under decentralization employees have more decision making authority.
   (b) Under decentralization, employees can identify customers tastes quickly.
   (c) Decentralization is more suited to organizations in stable environments.
   (d) Decentralized organizations are more adaptive.

2. The goals established by a responsibility center manager should be all of the following, EXCEPT:

   (a) specific.
   (b) measurable.
   (c) promote the long-term interests of the larger organization.
   (d) independent of other responsibility centers.

3. A flexible budget develops the cost target levels based on the:

   (a) actual level of activity.
   (b) standard level of activity.
   (c) historical level of activity.
   (d) pre-planned level of activity.

4. Managers of profit centers are responsible for:

   (a) costs and investments.
   (b) revenues and costs.
   (c) costs, revenues and investments.
   (d) revenues.

5. Many revenue centers control each of the following, EXCEPT:

   (a) sales price.
   (b) mix of stock carried.
   (c) promotional activities.
   (d) purchase of capital equipment.

6.   Probably the most significant problem in applying the controllability principle is that:

(a)   it is virtually impossible to determine what the manager is responsible for.
(b)   it applies only to very large responsibility centers.
(c)   many revenues and costs are jointly earned.
(d)   it applies only to very small responsibility centers

7.   Of the following transfer pricing methods which is set by the application of a rule or policy?

(a)   Administered transfer price.
(b)   Market-based transfer price.
(c)   Cost-based transfer price.
(d)   Negotiated transfer price.

8.   The biggest problem with cost-based transfers prices is:

(a)   they require too much negotiation.
(b)   they are very difficult to put in place
(c)   they are based on applications of simple rules.
(d)   there are too many cost possibilities and many will not provide the correct economic signal.

9.   If productivity is 1.45 operating income is $5,000,000, sales is $35,000,000 calculate ROI.

(a)   2.071%
(b)   21.00%
(c)   200.71%
(d)   10.15%

10.   If accounting income for Genis Company is 15% of sales, $5,000,000 of capital is used, the cost of capital is 8%, and sales is $12,000,000, what is residual income?

(a) $1,800,000
(b) $7,000,000
(c) $1,400,000
(d) $3,200,000

Solutions to Chapter Quiz/Demonstration Exercises _____

1. c.
2. d.
3. a.
4. b.
5. d.
6. c.
7. a.
8. d.
9. b.
10. c.

SYNOPSIS OF *READINGS IN MANAGEMENT ACCOUNTING* AND QUESTIONS TO ASSIGN WITH SUGGESTED ANSWERS

Synopsis of Readings in Management Accounting

The first two articles in this section focus on one of the central methods used for financial control -- flexible budgeting. Only very recently has there been discussion of how activity-based costing can be integrated with flexible budgeting; these article represent some of the most recent thinking on the subject.

Y. T. Mak and Melvin Roush's article, *"Flexible Budgeting and Variance Analysis in an Activity-Based Costing Environment"* (Reading 12.1) critiques several alternative views of how ABC affects traditional control methods such as flexible budgeting and variance analysis. They propose a framework for cost control under activity-based costing in which the traditional distinctions between fixed and variable costs are maintained. However, they propose that flexible budgets and variance analysis should be modified for each activity based on the underlying cost driver for that activity.

Robert S. Kaplan extends the discussion on flexible budgeting in Reading 2.2, *"Flexible Budgeting in an Activity-Based Costing Framework."* In this article, the distinction between the activity-based measurement of the costs of resources used and the conventional financial measurement of the costs of resources supplied is expanded to allow for the possibility that some portion of resources supplied to perform an activity could be committed, while another flexible portion is supplied as needed to meet actual demand for the activity. The paper extends previous thinking by outlining the principles for integrating activity-based costs into a flexible budgeting process and an ex post financial analysis of operating expenses.

Synopsis of Readings in Management Accounting

In Reading 12.3 *"Linking the Shop Floor to the Top Floor,"* Mark Beischel and Richard Smith present a integrative framework for linking manufacturing performance to overall company financial performance. Beischel and Smith state that the first task is to establish critical success factors for the organization that can be clearly measured. Every key aspect of a manufacturing process must be measured and each measure tied to a specific management level. As we go up the corporate hierarchy, the measures are combined into measures at the next level. Ultimately the entire set of measures in the organization must be linked to the critical success factor at the top of the organization (such as return on assets). The authors argue that, while nonfinancial measures of performance are important, all manufacturing performance measures should be tied, or subject to, some aspect of financial control. The message in this article is very important as many units or divisions of organizations develop critical success factors and performance measures for themselves, but often there is a failure to coordinate and integrate measures for the entire organization.

Points to Include in Answering Questions from the Readings

1.   What are the essential elements for controlling variable and fixed activity costs in Mak and Roush's article?

Student answers should include:
a.   For variable costs both price and efficiency variances can still be calculated. The price variance is the difference between actual costs and flexible budget costs based on the actual quantity of the cost driver. The efficiency variance is the difference between the flexible budget costs (based on actual quantity of the cost driver) and the flexible budget (based on standard quantity of the cost driver).
b.   For fixed costs both budget and capacity variances can still be calculated.   The budget variance is the difference between actual costs and budgeted activity spending based on the availability of the cost driver. The capacity variance is the difference between budgeted activity spending (based on availability of the cost driver) and the budgeted activity usage (based on standard quantity of the cost driver).

2a.   In Kaplan's article, how are the costs of resources used related to the costs of resources supplied?

Student answers should include:
a.   Costs of resources supplied =
        costs of resources used + cost of unused capacity.

2b.   When the resources used/resources supplied distinction is incorporated into an activity-based costing framework, is there still an inconsistency with periodic financial performance measurement?

Student answers should include:
a.   Traditionally, periodic financial statements only measured the costs of resources supplied, and activity-based costs were aggregated into the costs of resources used.   If   both elements on the right-hand side of the equation in 2a are included there is no longer an inconsistency.

Points to Include in Answering Questions from the Readings

3.   According to Beischel and Smith, what are five critical success factors that should be measured and how are they defined?

Student answers should include:
a.   Quality - meeting or exceeding customer needs and achieving customer satisfaction.
b.   Customer service - External service is meeting customer demand for end-products, while internal service is meeting the demands of other internal customers.
c.   Resource management - optimizing output to inputs in people, inventory and fixed capital.
d.   Cost - the costs that can be managed at the level reported.
e.   flexibility - responsiveness to changing market, regulatory and environmental demands.

Recommended Cases

1.   Both Lynchburgh Foundry and Birch Paper Company in Rotch, Allen and Smith, are good cases to use for transfer pricing.

2.   Polysar Ltd (Harvard Case 9-187-098; teaching note 5-187-198) presents issues related to budgeting, capacity planning, profit centers and performance measures.

3.   Siemens Electric Motor Works (A) and (B) (HBS case 9-189-089 and 9-189-090 and teaching notes 5-189-127 and 5-189-128) explores the link between ABC and transfer pricing.

For more background, I would also recommend reviewing a well-known article by John Dearden, "The Case Against ROI Control," *Harvard Business Review* 47 (May-June, 1969), pp. 124-135.

In addition, Shawn Tully's article, "The Real Key to Creating Wealth," in *Readings in Management Accounting*, Chapter 13 can also be assigned with this chapter.

CHAPTER 13

Compensation

CENTRAL FOCUS AND LEARNING OBJECTIVES

Issues related to compensation are discussed in this chapter. These include:

1. The importance of understanding the role of motivation in organizations

2. The elements of two important theories of motivation

3. The different approaches to rewarding performance and the nature of intrinsic and extrinsic rewards

4. The characteristics of effective reward systems

5. The guidelines that organizations might use to design reward systems

6. The broad types of monetary rewards that organizations use

Chapter Overview

Chapter 13 addresses the role of compensation in organizational control. Compensation is a central issue in many types of organizations and is tied in closely with management control and organizational design issues.

Beginning with theories of individual motivation by Herzberg and Vroom, factors that affect motivation such as working conditions, base pay, organization policies achievement, recognition, opportunities for growth and a number of others are presented. Controversial issues such as whether intrinsic or extrinsic rewards are the most motivating and how rewards are tied to performance also are debated.

Another set of issues related to what constitutes effective performance measurement and reward systems are addressed. In the final section the advantages and disadvantages of the major types of incentive compensation plans such as cash bonuses, profit sharing, gain sharing and stock options and stock-related compensation plans are discussed.

Chapter Outline _____

 Designing incentive systems for employees in organizations has become a controversial topic. You might point out to students that some of the controversy stems from the very high salaries that many CEOs have been making in the United States over the past decade. Another part of the controversy, which is discussed in Alfie Kohn's article, is that some believe the use of financial rewards may create an environment in which achieving the reward is the goal and not building the organization for the long-term.

Learning Objective 1: The importance of understanding the role of motivation in organizations (this is an umbrella heading and no multiple choice questions are suggested).

Learning Objective 2: The elements of 2 important theories of motivation. DO MULTIPLE CHOICE QUESTIONS 1 and 2.

I.   The Role of Compensation in Organizational Control

This chapter will discuss a number of central issues relating to compensation beginning with two well-known theories of individual motivation.

   1.   **Hygiene factors** are those necessary to provide the appropriate environment for motivation rather than motivation itself.

   2.   **Satisfier factors** provide motivation when the environment for motivation has been properly prepared

B.   Vroom's Expectancy Theory

   1.   **Expectancy theory** argues that motivation is a product of expectancy, instrumentality, and valence.

a. **Expectancy** is the relationship that a person perceives between effort and skill and whether these will achieve the targeted performance.

b. **Instrumentality** is the relationship between measured performance and the outcomes provided to individuals.

c. A **valence** is the value that a person assigns to the outcomes provided by the organization as a result of formal performance measurement.

2. A **motivation system** is a performance measurement system and reward system that provides employee benefits or recognition based on measured performance.

 Exhibits 13-2 and 13-3 illustrate Herzberg's and Vroom's theories. Ask students what the key differences are.

Learning Objective 3: The different approaches to rewarding performance and the nature of intrinsic and extrinsic rewards. DO MULTIPLE CHOICE QUESTIONS 3 and 4.

Readings in Management Accounting

Alfie Kohn's "Why Incentive Plans Cannot Work," (Reading 13.1) discusses critically many aspects of incentives and particularly the assumptions underlying incentive plans.

II.   Factors Affecting Individual Motivation

Organizations use two broad categories of rewards to motivate people:

A.   **Intrinsic rewards** are those relating to the nature of the organization and the design of the job, that people experience without the intervention of anyone else. These rewards come from inside the individual and include satisfaction and feelings of accomplishment.

B.   **Extrinsic rewards** are those based on performance that are provided to the individual by the organization. These include trips, financial rewards, employee awards, etc.

C.   The issue of what types and mix of rewards (intrinsic versus extrinsic rewards) varies considerably and there are numerous debates on the issue. On the one hand some argue that not enough emphasis is placed on developing an environment from which intrinsic rewards for individuals can be derived. Others claim that extrinsic rewards are the most motivating types of rewards and that people respond best to money and external recognition that is based on their performance. Each organization must decide on the type of work environment it would like to develop and the mix of both types of rewards.

III.   Rewards Based on Performance

Incentive compensation or pay-for-performance is a system that provides rewards for performance to motivate achieving, or exceeding, measured performance targets.

A.   Rewards can be based on *absolute performance* as in piece-rate incentive schemes for the number of good products produced.

B.   Rewards also can be based on relative performance such as paying the top insurance salesperson a bonus each month.

Learning Objective 4: The characteristics of effective reward systems. DO MULTIPLE CHOICE QUESTIONS 5 and 6.

Readings in Management Accounting

Jeffrey Kerr and John Slocum's "Managing Corporate Culture Through Reward Systems," (Reading 13.2) presents an overview of the relationship between reward systems and the values and norms that make up corporate culture.

IV.   Effective Performance Measurement and Reward Systems

  A.   If the organization has decided to reward performance, five broad characteristics should be considered to ensure that the performance measurement system will be effective.

  1.   Individuals must understand their jobs and know how to improve their performance.

  2.   The reward system has to be understandable and employees have to be able to see how improved performance will affect rewards.

  3.   The reward system has to measure the employee's controllable performance and minimize or eliminate uncontrollable factors.

  4.   The measurement system must measure the objects of measurement systematically and accurately.

  5.   In some instances, incentives should consider rewarding groups, rather than individuals where appropriate.

 Ask students whether all of the above conditions were present in the last job (full-time or part-time) that they had.

B.   Conditions Favoring Incentive Compensation

Incentive compensation seems to work best in decentralized systems where employees are empowered and can use their skill and authority to react to situations and make decisions.

C.   Incentive Compensation and Employee Responsibility

An employee's compensation should reflect the nature of his or her responsibilities. For instance those who work in daily operations should have rewards that are tied to short-term measures such as customer service, those who work on intermediate term projects should be rewarded based on meeting budgets, and finally those who work on long-term projects should be rewarded on measures such as long-term growth or process improvements.

D.   Rewarding Outcomes

Employees provide two types of inputs to an organization. These are time and skill. Incentive system designers usually look to the outputs of employees as measures of how employees use their inputs on the job. As employees bring more skill and experience to a job they are rewarded with some form of knowledge-based pay. Thus, employees are encouraged to keep upgrading their skills.

E.   Managing Incentive Compensation Plans

There is controversy over the management of compensation plans especially at the senior executive level. The criticism is that senior executives have been overpaid for mediocre performance. This perceived unfairness has tended to discourage lower-level employees beliefs that incentive compensation systems are equitable.

Learning Objective 5: The guidelines that organizations might use to design reward systems DO MULTIPLE CHOICE QUESTION 5

F. Guidelines for Effective Incentive Compensation Systems

There are four broad guidelines for developing incentive compensation systems:

1. Fairness - this relates to the idea that the highest paid person in the organization should be paid no more than twenty times the total pay of the lowest person. This has been violated dramatically in the United States.

2. Participation - if organizations use incentive compensation all employees should be allowed to participate in a plan.

3. Basic Wage Level - each employee should be paid a basic wage that reflects the market value of the employee's skills and experience. Incentive compensation should not be a substitute for the basic wage.

4. Independent Wage Policy - the Board of Directors' Compensation Committee should set senior management's compensation and not senior management.

G. Issues in Designing Incentive Compensation Plans

Key issues in Design include:

1. What performance should be measured?

2. What are the appropriate standards against which to compare performance?

3. Should compensation be based on individual or group performance?

4. What should be the form of monetary rewards (cash, perquisites, or equity)?

5. Should rewards be deferred or paid immediately?

Readings in Management Accounting

Shawn Tully's article, "The Real Key to Creating Wealth," (Reading 13.3) explores the financial tool known as economic value added (EVA).

So much is written in the business press about incentive compensation that you might ask students, as an assignment, to bring in and critique an article that discusses one of the following types of incentive plans listed below.

H.   Types of Incentive Compensation Plans

1.   A **cash bonus,** or a lump sum reward, is a cash award based on some measured performance. Cash bonuses, which can be based on individual or group performance, are given when performance exceeds a target

2.   **Profit-sharing** is a cash bonus system where the total amount available for distribution as cash bonuses is a function of the organization's, or an organization unit's, reported profit. Thus, profit-sharing is a group incentive plan.

3.   **Gainsharing** is another group incentive system where the total amount available for distribution as cash bonuses is a function of performance relative to some target (usually the difference between the actual and the target level of labor cost).

The three most widely used gainsharing programs are:

A.   Improshare (Improved Productivity Sharing) determines its bonus pool by calculating the difference between the target level of labor cost given the level of production and the actual labor cost.

B.   Scanlon Plans

First a base ratio is calculated using past data.

$$\text{Base ratio} = \frac{\text{payroll costs}}{\text{value of production or service}}$$

In any period in which the ratio of payroll costs are less than the base ratio, the labor savings are added to the bonus pool.

C.   Rucker Plan

The Rucker plan also works on a ratio based on past data.

$$\text{Rucker standard} = \frac{\text{payroll costs}}{\text{production value}}$$

where production value = (net sales - inventory change - materials and supplies used).

Similar to the Scanlon plan, when actual labor costs are less than the Rucker standard, its employees receive a bonus.

4. A **stock option** is a right to purchase a stated number of the organization's shares at a stipulated price (the option price).

The general idea behind stock options is to motivate employees to act in the long-run interests of the organization by taking actions and making decisions that will increase the organization's market value.

Chapter Quiz/Demonstration Exercises _____

1.   In Herzberg's Theory of motivation, recognition is:

   (a)   an expectancy.
   (b)   a hygiene factor.
   (c)   a satisfier factor.
   (d)   a valence.

2.   In Vroom's Expectancy Theory, a valence is:

   (a)   the individual's expectations about whether the application
           of skill and effort will achieve the targeted performance.
   (b)   the relationship between the individual's measured
           performance and the outcomes provided by the
           organization.
   (c)   an extrinsic reward.
   (d)   the value assigned by the individual to the outcomes.

3.   Which of the following is not an extrinsic reward?

   (a)   A cash bonus.
   (b)   Feeling like you have done a good job.
   (c)   Being named employee of the month and having your name
           on a plaque.
   (d)   Being given a trip to Cleveland as a prize.

4.   In the Kohn article discussed in Chapter 13, Kohn argues that
           _____ rewards have been overemphasized while _____
        rewards have been largely ignored.

   (a)   instrinsic, extrinsic
   (b)   stock option, cash bonus
   (c)   extrinsic, intrinsic
   (d)   cash bonus, stock option

5. Which of the following is not part of the effective design of a performance measurement and reward system?

(a) The reward system must set clear standards for performance that the employee can accept.
(b) The reward system has to measure the employee's controllable performance.
(c) Making sure all employees know their jobs.
(d) The reward system must also be based on the performance of the individual.

6. Which of the following types of organizations are least suited for incentive compensation?

(a) Highly centralized organizations.
(b) Highly decentralized organizations.
(c) Organizations that face quickly changing environments.
(d) Organizations in which employees have a great deal of decision making responsibility.

7. Each of the following is a broad, long-standing guideline for the development of effective incentive compensation systems, EXCEPT:

(c) An independent wage policy that does not allow senior management to set its own wage and incentive compensation system.
(a) A fair system in which the highest paid employee should not earn more than 20 times the lowest paid person.
(b) Participation of all employees in the incentive plan.
(d) A basic wage level, unless the organization uses incentive compensation and then the wage level should be reduced.

8. Under the Rucker plan, the Rucker standard is:

(a) Payroll costs/inventory value.
(b) Net cash inflow/Value of production or service.
(c) Payroll costs/production value.
(d) Net cash inflow/Net sales.

9. Under the Scanlon plan, Neuf Company's base ratio is 0.36. If payroll costs are $7,000,000 and the value of production is $20,000,000 how much money is added to the bonus pool?

(a) $2,520,000
(b) $200,000.
(c) $0.
(d) $4,680,000.

10. A stock option is the right to purchase a unit of the organization's stock, at a specified price called the _____ _____.

(a) discount price.
(b) premium price.
(c) purchase price.
(d) option price.

Solutions to Chapter Quiz/Demonstration Exercises _____

1.   c.
2.   d.
3.   b.
4.   c.
5.   d.
6.   a.
7.   d.
8.   c.
9.   b.
10. d.

SYNOPSIS OF *READINGS IN MANAGEMENT ACCOUNTING* AND QUESTIONS TO ASSIGN WITH SUGGESTED ANSWERS

Synopsis of Readings in Management Accounting

The readings in this section begin with a controversial article by Alfie Kohn. Alfie Kohn's "*Why Incentive Plans Cannot Work*" (Reading 13.1), argues strongly that incentive plans that link rewards to measured performance are fundamentally flawed. Citing research evidence, Kohn believes that employees who expect to receive a reward for their efforts do not perform as well as those who do not expect rewards. What is lacking with current pay-for-performance systems is that they do not foster a work environment in which employees can experience intrinsic rewards. Ultimately, the preoccupation with extrinsic rewards does not lead to organizational commitment, discourages risk taking, and reduces creativity and innovation.

Another manifestation of the way that organizations set up their rewards system is discussed in Jeffrey Kerr and John Slocum's article, "*Managing Corporate Culture Through Reward Systems*" (Reading 13.2). Kerr and Slocum believe that the kinds of reward systems that organizations use will dictate the corporate culture. They state that: "The reward system -- who gets rewarded and why -- is an unequivocal statement of the corporation's values and beliefs." Using data collected from 14 firms, the authors identified two distinct types of reward systems -- a hierarchy-based system, and a performance-based system each of which led to a different kind of organizational culture. Kerr and Slocum suggest that, in many cases, rewards are such powerful mechanisms that the redesign of an incentive system can change an organization's culture.

Synopsis of Readings in Management Accounting

Shawn Tully's article, "*The Real Key to Creating Wealth*" (Reading 13.3), describes one of the most popular business tools called economic value added (EVA). EVA has become extremely popular as a measure of profitability since it includes the total cost of an organization's capital in the measure. Stated another way, EVA is after-tax operating profit less the total annual cost of capital. The most significant difference between EVA and other measures is that, with EVA, the cost of both borrowed capital and equity capital is included in the calculation. Most previous methods ignored the potentially expensive cost of equity capital. Because EVA focuses on the valued-added concept, many managerial compensation systems (that include bonus and stock plans) now are being developed based on EVA. Such incentive systems may overcome many of the problems of bonus systems based on short-term earnings that both Kohn and Kerr and Slocum discuss.

Points to Include in Answering Questions from the Readings

1.   What are the six reasons that incentive programs fail, according to Alfie Kohn?

Student answers should include:
a.   Pay is not a motivator - research shows that employees tend to care about other factors, pay ranks 5th or 6th on the list.
b.   Rewards punish - rewards can be just as manipulative as punishment.
c.   Rewards rupture relationships - forcing people to compete for rewards can have many negative effects, including putting individuals ahead of groups and the organization.
d.   Rewards ignore reason - relying on rewards to boost productivity often does not get at the underlying reasons why productivity is low.
e.   Rewards discourage risk-taking - rewards reduce creativity as employees want to continue what they know how to do to achieve the rewards.
f.   Rewards undermine interest - stressing money over intrinsic rewards may divert a person's interest to the reward and away from the work.

Points to Include in Answering Questions from the Readings

2.   In Kerr and Slocum's article, what are the characteristics of hierarchy-based reward systems and performance-based systems? What kinds of corporate culture does each promote?

Student answers should include:
I.   In hierarchy-based systems:

a.   Superiors define and evaluate the performance of subordinates.
b.   Performance is defined both quantitatively and qualitatively.

Points to Include in Answering Questions from the Readings

    c.   Nonquantifiable aspects of the subordinate's role were sometimes considered more important than quantifiable ones.

    d.   Superiors interpreted the performance of subordinates according to subjective criteria.

    e.   Managers' jobs were broadly and subtly defined.

    f.   Bonuses were based on corporate performance and thus the team and not individuals were rewarded.

    g.   Promotion from within was the standard policy.

II.   In performance-based systems

    a.   Performance was objectively defined and measured.

    b.   Qualitative aspects were ignored.

    c.   Specific rewards or proportions of rewards were directly related to specific performance criteria.

    d.   The manager's job was specifically defined.

    e.   There was little subjectivity involved in performance evaluation.

    f.   The bonus system rewarded individual performance.

    g.   Promoting from within was not the norm.

3.   According to Tully, what are the key questions that a manager has to ask to determine his or her EVA?

Student answers should include:

    a.   What's the true cost of your capital? Both the cost of borrowed capital and equity capital must be included.

    b.   How much capital is tied up in your operation? This includes what you paid for real estate, machines, vehicles plus working capital.

Recommended Cases

1. Provigo, Inc. (A), (B) and (C) (HBS case numbers 9-189-105, 9-189-106 and 9-189-107; teaching note for all three cases 5-190-081). This is a comprehensive three-part case on incentive compensation issues such as the design of incentive plans, goal setting and budgeting.

2. GTE Corp.: Long-Term Incentive Program (HBS case 9-191-005). This case illustrates the difficulties with a long-term incentive plan.

3. Nordstrom: Dissension in the Ranks (A) (HBS case 9-191-002; teaching note 5-692-085). The case describes a highly competitive compensation system for sales employees.

Chapter 14

Behavioral and Organizational Issues in Management Accounting and Control System Design

CENTRAL FOCUS AND LEARNING OBJECTIVES

This chapter emphasizes many of the behavioral issues involved with MACS system design and functioning. The chapter's learning objectives are to discuss:

1. Managerial approaches to motivation, and in particular, the Human Resources Model

2. The characteristics of well-designed MACS and the links among the concepts of motivation, ethics, control and performance and the design of management accounting and control systems (MACS)

3. The behavioral consequences of poorly designed MACS

4. The human factors to consider when changing and implementing a new MACS

Chapter Overview _____

Chapter 14 presents an in-depth discussion of a number of behavioral and organizational issues related to the design of management accounting and control systems (MACS). The chapter begins with a presentation of three major schools of thought on how management views human motivation. The three schools discussed are Scientific Management, Human Relations and Human Resources.

The Human Resource Model is the one around which the chapter is built. This particular model, a synthesis of concepts from the Human Relations Movement and Japanese management methods, relies heavily on the value of employees to the organization. With this view all employees are thought of as significant contributors to the organization through their creativity and desire to work.

Thus, the MACS should be designed congruent with this view of human motivation. Five key ideas are central for a well-designed MACS. First, a multiple perspectives approach should be adopted. This means that the organization develops an integrated system that is consistent at a global level, but allows for a great deal of flexibility at local levels. Another central idea is the incorporation of an ethical code of conduct. Other key concepts such as the importance of quantitative and qualitative information, the participation and empowerment of employees and reward systems tied to performance round out the characteristics of a well-designed MACS. The chapter also discusses behaviors such as smoothing, gaming and data falsification that arise when a MACS is poorly designed. The final topic concerns variables that must be managed when a new MACS is installed in an organization.

Chapter Outline _____

> The material in this chapter covers a number of behavioral topics. Usually, I stress to students that modern management accounting has strong economic and behavioral consequences. Typically textbooks focus on the economic issues and ignore the behavioral side, but more and more the importance of the link between behavioral science and management accounting is becoming of critical importance, especially regarding implementation of new MACS.

I.   The goals of a management accounting and control system (MACS) are:

   A.   **Planning** for the future.

   B.   **Monitoring** events in the external environment.

   C.   **Measuring** and **recording** the results of activities occurring inside the organization.

   D.   **Motivating** individuals and groups who are affected by and who affect the MACS.

   E.   **Evaluating the performance** of individuals and groups in the organization.

> **Learning Objective 1. Managerial approaches to motivation. DO MULTIPLE CHOICE QUESTIONS 1 AND 2.**

II. In contrast to the individual models of motivation discussed in Chapter 13 there are three major managerial approaches to motivation. These are:

   A.   **Scientific Management** - a school of motivation in which people were viewed as finding work objectionable, motivated only money and have little knowledge to contribute to the organization.

B. **Human Relations Movement** -model of human motivation that considers that people have many needs and aspirations at work, and that they are motivated by things other than money.

C. **The Human Resources Model** - an approach to human motivation that emphasizes that individuals do not find work objectionable, that they have knowledge to contribute, and that they creative.

Learning Objective 2: Characteristics of a well-designed MACS and the links among motivation, ethics, control and performance. DO MULTIPLE CHOICE QUESTIONS 3, 4 and 5.

 In practice, there may be very few MACS with all five of the following characteristics. However, many organizations are striving to incorporate these characteristics. In essence, the chapter is presenting a normative model of MACS design.

III. The five key characteristics of a MACS:

A. The **multiple perspectives approach** provides for a consistent, organization-wide management accounting system that also allows for local input and tailoring.

 The study of ethics and ethical behavior has assumed great importance in all aspects of business. That importance is reflected both in the chapter and readings material.

Readings in Management Accounting

Two readings can be assigned for the material on ethics. These are, R. M. Boisjoly, "Personal Integrity and Accountability," (with the Preface by Jerry Arnold) (Reading 14.1), and K. Labich, "The New Crisis in Business Ethics." (Reading 14.2). Mr. Boisjoly's article is highly illustrative of the importance of living one's life through ethical principles. Mr. Labich's article stresses how the difficulties of managing in these tough times has led to an increase in unethical behavior and ties in nicely to the non-goal congruent behaviors of smoothing, gaming and data falsification discussing later in the chapter.

B. A system that reinforces the **ethical responsibilities** of all firm employees. Most organizations attempt to avoid ethical dilemmas by developing a code of ethics. *Note that this is one of several hierarchies that organizations can use.*

1. A **hierarchy of ethical principles** listed below, captures the broad array of ethical considerations.

   a. legal rules
   b. societal norms
   c. professional memberships (CPAs, CMAs, etc.)
   d. organizational or group norms
   e. personal norms

2. **Dealing With Ethical Conflicts.** Different kinds of conflicts can arise for employees in an organization. These include:

   a. conflicts between individual and organization values
   b. conflicts between the organization's stated and practiced values. Alternative four, *delay taking action and work with respected leaders in the organization to change the*

discrepancy in the text is one that is often recommended to be tried first.

3.   The Elements of an Effective Ethical Control System are:

    a.   A **statement** of the organization's values and code of ethics that is stated in practical terms, and that uses examples.

    b.   A clear statement of the employee's **ethical responsibilities** for every job description.

    c.   Adequate training to help employees identify ethical dilemmas in practice and learn how to deal with those dilemmas.

    d.   Evidence that senior management expects organization members to **adhere** to its code of ethics.

    e.   Evidence that employees can make ethical decisions, or report violations of the organizations stated ethics without fear of **reprisals** from superiors, subordinates, or peers in the organization.

    f.   Providing for an ongoing **internal audit** of the efficacy of the organization's ethical control system.

Readings in Management Accounting

Reading 14.3 by J. Fisher, "Use of Nonfinancial Performance Measures," can be used at this juncture. The article discusses how several high tech manufacturing plants implemented nonfinancial measures of performance and the problems and opportunities that resulted.

C.   The development and use of both **quantitative and qualitative information** in a timely fashion for control, motivation, and performance evaluation.

1. Quantitative measures include financial measures such as net income and physical measures such as number of units produced.

2. Qualitative measures include image and reputation.

D. The **participation and empowerment of employees** in system design and improvements, and continuous education of employees in understanding how the system functions and how the information can be interpreted meaningfully.

   1. **Employee Empowerment** means providing employees the ability to affect their work environment through more discretion and autonomy.

   2. **Participation** in budget and decision-making is a joint decision making process in which all parties jointly decide on the levels of the budget. **Imposition** of the budget occurs when a superior simply tells a subordinate what his or her budget will be, without any input from the subordinate.

Stress that "true" participation has to be a jointly negotiated process and not one in which the employee submits a budget and waits to see what senior management decides.

E. Development of mechanisms such as **reward systems** tied to performance to promote motivation and goal congruence between the organization and employees to reduce dysfunctional behavior.

Learning Objective 3: Behavioral consequences of poorly designed MACS. DO MULTIPLE CHOICE QUESTIONS 6 AND 7.

IV.   Behavioral Consequences of Poorly Designed Systems include:

 Ask students if they have ever engaged in any of the behaviors listed below.

   A.   Behaviors that are not goal congruent with the organization. Goal congruence is the alignment of individual and organization's goals. Types of non-goal congruent behavior include:

      1.   **Smoothing** occurs when an employee alters the pre-planned flow of information without altering actual behavior.

      2.   **Gaming** occurs when an employee alters his or her planned actions as a result of a particular kind of performance indicator.

         a.   Building **budget slack**, or excess resources above what are needed to accomplish the goals set forth in the budget, is an example of gaming.

      3.   **Data falsification** is the act of knowingly falsifying information

Learning Objective 4: Human factors to consider when implementing a new MACS. DO MULTIPLE CHOICE QUESTIONS 8, 9, AND 10.

 From visits to many organizations, the issues discussed below keep surfacing every time there are changes to the MACS. Many of the concerns about change can only be overcome with the help of professional change agents helping to lead the changes. This is not to say that organizational members cannot foment change, it's just that many do not have the professional experience or know-how to get employees to accept and commit to change.

V.   Behavioral considerations when implementing new MACS include:

A.   Before changes to the MACS are made, organizations often use **cooperative benchmarking** (some prefer to call this competitive benchmarking, although, the term cooperative seems to have taken hold most recently) to compare and borrow information about how others have designed their systems. Cooperative benchmarking involves comparing and borrowing the best practices from other organizations.

B.   Knowledge of **organizational culture** is another key element in changing systems. Organizational culture can be defined as the mindset of organizational participants including goals, values and attitude. There are many types of cultures including:

1.   **strong, functional cultures** with well defined goals, values and a great deal of employee involvement and goal congruence.

2.   **strong, dysfunctional cultures** that are usually characterized by top-down control and little employee involvement and very little goal congruence.

3.   **Ill-defined cultures** in which employees do not have well defined goals and do not have a sense of corporate mission. Goal congruence is usually low.

Readings in Management Accounting

S. Mark Young's, "A Framework for Successful Adoption and Performance of Japanese Manufacturing Practices in the United States," (Reading 14.4) discusses numerous issues involved with importing manufacturing practices from another culture without thinking through all of the ramifications. Both primary and secondary control are discussed in-depth.

C. Knowledge of current manufacturing and service practices and control methods. Organizations that have tried to implement JIT systems have often not taken into account the difference between primary and secondary control systems and as a result have met with resistance. *A key point to make is that just knowing how to implement the technical side of a system is not sufficient for success. If the designers do not realize what kind of environment and culture they are dealing with then implementation problems and resistance can be significant.*

1. **Primary Control** is a method of control in which employees further their own ends by trying to influence their environment.

2. **Secondary Control** is a method of control in which employees adapt themselves to their environment, rather than trying to change the environment.

3. A **champion** is an individual who takes the initiative and risk to develop a new management accounting system.

4. The **change Process** consists of the procedures and actions by which change is implemented.

    A. **Resistance to Change** can arise when an employee refuses to accept the changes brought about in an organization some of these reasons are:

        i. people are set in their ways.
        ii. change can be costly in terms lost compensation for some employees.
        iii. if the scope of change is large, there may be a great deal of lost time or downtime.
        iv. change can shift the power base in the organization.

    B. **Resistance to ABC/ABM**, in particular may also occur because:
        i. activity analysis can reveal how employees are really spending their time.

      ii.   some employees associate ABC/ABM with cost cutting and they are afraid that they will lose their jobs.

5. **Commitment** is the implicit pledging of organizational participants to a course of action.

6. **Continuous Education** is a commitment on the part of the organization to provide educational programs for employees on an on-going basis.

7. **Compensation** consists of financial incentives to promote desired behavior.

Chapter Quiz/Demonstration Exercises_____

1.   The Human Resources Model of motivation:

      a.   was strongly influenced by Herzberg's theory
      b.   was strongly influenced by Vroom's theory
      c.   was strongly influenced by Japanese management methods
      d.   was strongly influenced by the multiple perspective approach

2.   The Human Relations Movement began:

      a.   at the beginning of the 1960's
      b.   at the beginning of the 1900's
      c.   during the late 1950's
      d.   during the late 1930's

3.   When designing a MACS all of the following are important EXCEPT:

      a.   participation and empowerment of employees should be avoided.
      b.   development and use of both quantitative and qualitative information.
      c.   use of the multiple perspectives approach to system design.
      d.   reward systems tied to performance

4.   Ethical codes of conduct are:

      a.   mandatory in all U.S. business organizations.
      b.   part of a well-designed MACS.
      c.   mandatory just for "for-profit" organizations
      d.   not important for any organization.

5.   Rewards are often tied to performance because:

      a.   such a system is very easy to design.
      b.   all employees are naturally lazy
      c.   motivation for employees is thought to increase.
      d.   it always increases net income for the firm.

6. Three examples of non-goal congruent behavior are:

    a.   smoothing, gaming and benchmarking
    b.   gaming, data falsification and resisting
    c.   Data falsification, gaming and sifting
    d.   smoothing, gaming and data falsification

7. Budget participation can have the following effects, EXCEPT:

    a.   decrease the possibility of gaming.
    b.   increase job satisfaction.
    c.   lead to budget slack.
    d.   increase employee morale

8. Organizational culture can be described as:

    a.   The vision of top management
    b.   The mindset of employees, including their shared beliefs, values and goals.
    c.   The mindset of all managers.
    d..   The mindset of employees, except those who are hourly paid workers.

9. Continuous education:

    a.   is now mandatory in all manufacturing firms.
    b.   costs about 5% of an organization's operating budget.
    c.   can improve employees skills.
    d.   will not improve employee commitment.

10. A change champion:

    a.   must gain the support of top management.
    b.   does not need financial support, just motivation.
    c.   can usually implement the changes by him or herself.
    d.   has to come from the finance organization.

SOLUTIONS TO CHAPTER QUIZ/DEMONSTRATION EXERCISES

1. c
2. d
3. a
4. b
5. c
6. d
7. a
8 b
9. c
10. a

SYNOPSIS OF *READINGS IN MANAGEMENT ACCOUNTING* AND QUESTIONS TO ASSIGN WITH SUGGESTED ANSWERS

Synopsis of Readings in Management Accounting

The readings in this chapter cover several different topics including ethical control, the use of financial and nonfinancial performance measures, and cultural issues relating to the design of management accounting and control system design. Reading 14.1, Roger Boisjoly's article "*Personal Integrity and Accountability*," is a very personal and powerful account of the author's ethical decision to come forward and testify before a Presidential Commission against NASA and Morton Thikol, Inc. for knowingly launching the Space Shuttle Challenger when there were strong recommendations against doing so. Coming forward ultimately cost Mr. Boisjoly his health and his career, but he is very clear that he did the right thing.

Kenneth Labich's "*The New Crisis in Business Ethics*" (Reading 14.2) discusses how the issues of personal integrity and ethical conduct discussed by Mr. Boisjoly are being tested on a very large scale in U.S. business today. Given difficult economic times, many companies are competing more fiercely. Corporate survival has placed employees under great pressure to achieve corporate objectives, in many cases without regard to maintaining their ethical standards. However, apart from the personal cost of engaging in unethical behavior, the financial cost can be staggering for those who get caught and convicted of antitrust violations, breaking securities laws, fraud, bribery, etc. To educate their employees, approximately 200 major U.S. corporations have appointed ethics officers and many are conducting ethics workshops and seminars.

On a different topic, Joe Fisher's "*Use of Nonfinancial Performance Measures*" (Reading 14.3) examines the implementation of nonfinancial measures and control at five high-technology plants. Based on his study of these plants, Fisher develops a six-phase model of the implementation process. The companies that were studied also pointed to problems that they had had with their traditional accounting systems which ultimately led them to develop nonfinancial measures of performance. Fisher describes a number of these problems as well as the strengths and weaknesses of the nonfinancial measures that companies use.

Synopsis of Readings in Management Accounting

In "*A Framework for Successful Adoption and Performance of Japanese Manufacturing Practices in the United States,*" (Reading 14.4), S. Mark Young discusses another topic related to the design of management accounting and control systems. Studying the issue of adopting six factors relating to Japanese manufacturing practices in the United States, Young suggests each factor cannot simply be implemented without consideration of how it will affect the work environment. Young develops a framework for successful implementation and suggests ways that both the practices and the work environment can be modified to accommodate each of the manufacturing methods.

Points to Include in Answering Questions from the Readings

1. Write an essay describing what you have would have done if you were in Mr. Boisjoly's position.

    Class approach:

    I think that you may get a wide range of responses on this essay. Some will say that they would have done what Boisjoly did, while others will say that NASA and MTI took a calculated risk and lost. You may want to pick two essays that are diametrically opposed and explore the issues with the class. Another powerful example that you may wish to use is the movie "The China Syndrome." Jack Lemmon blows the whistle on a nuclear power plant that has serious problems. Most management and operating personnel believe that there is something wrong, but are so intent on opening the plant and begin to recoup their investment that they are willing to take the risk of a meltdown. You might wish to show clips from the movie or ask someone who has seen it to discuss the parallels to the Challenger situation.

Points to Include in Answering Questions from the Readings

2. Based on Labich's article, write an essay addressing the question: "Are there any conditions under which you would engage in unethical behavior?"

    Class approach:

    In a similar vein to question 1, I would pick two essays and read them anonymously and engage students in a debate. Another alternative is to compile a list of reasons why students would engage in unethical behavior. Put the list on the board and have students debate each one. I think you will find this to be a very lively class!

3. What are the deficiencies of traditional accounting systems that led the companies studied by Fisher to adopt nonfinancial measures?

    Student answers should include:
    a. Variances not actionable at the operating level - difficulty in tracing a variance to a specific problem.
    b. Numbers too summarized and on too aggregate a level - no clear connections between managers' actions and monthly reports.
    c. Overreliance on labor or machine hours - problems exacerbated with the use of volume-based overhead rules.
    d. Dysfunctional activities - the goal of maximizing an individual variance may lead to dysfunctional activities for the firm as a whole.
    e. Setting standards - costly and difficult process and often out-of-date.
    f. Conflicts with continuous improvement - standard setting often interferes with continuous improvement.
    g. Lack of timely signals - variances calculated once a month and disseminated two weeks later; information was deemed useless.

Points to Include in Answering Questions from the Readings

4.   What are the six factors relating to Japanese manufacturing practices that Young discusses? Describe the variables that have to be managed with each of the six practices for successful implementation in the U.S. to occur.

Student answers should include:
a.   Kaizen
            - layoff policies
            - type of reward
b.   Kanban
            - pace of work
            - lack of discipline
c.   Total Quality Control
            - level of responsibility
            - team orientation
            - level of skills of workers
d.   JIT Purchasing
            - vendor location
            - vendor incentives and training
e.   Secondary Control
            - work rules
            - group orientation
            - training programs
            - union sentiment and plant location

Recommended Cases

1.   Disctech Inc. (HBS case #9-187-066; teaching note 5-187-180. This case is about fraudulent information manipulation by managers who had the support of top management.   This is an excellent case to use to discuss ethical issues.

2.   Graves Industries (A), (B), (C) and video (HBS case numbers 9-187-045; 9-187-046; 9-187-047; teaching note 5-187-179 for cases A-C; video 9-887-529).   These cases depict events occurring over a three year period that led to fraudulent financial reporting.   A very good series on ethics.

3.   Zytec Corporation (B) (HBS case 190-066; teaching note 5-191-206). This case has several foci, but can be used to illustrate how to design a cost system to modify behavior.

4.   Tektronix: Portable Instruments Division (A) and (B) HBS Case 188-142 and 188-143; teaching note 5-191-189.   Both the Tektronix cases discuss the implications of changing to more advanced cost management systems and the behavioral effects of such changes.